Praise for *Excellent Protestant Congregations*

"Paul Wilkes is a perceptive observer who has found encouraging evidence of robust health, vigor, and diversity among today's churches. This book will give you a wider field of vision—and a glimpse of what God is doing in America's churches."

—Marshall Shelley, editor, *Leadership Journal*
and www.christianitytoday.com

"*Excellent Protestant Congregations* is not a book of easy answers that are supposed to work everywhere. But every pastor, seminarian, and committed layperson will find something to use in its pages, and all of us will find much to celebrate. The book is a spirited tour of the diversity and vitality in Protestant congregations today."

—Robin Lovin, Dean, Perkins School of Theology,
Southern Methodist University

"This book, along with Wilkes's companion volume *Excellent Catholic Parishes*, should be must-reading for pastors, lay leaders, seminary faculty, students, or anyone interested in congregational vitality. I cannot commend it too strongly!"

—Jackson Carroll, author of *Mainline to the Future: Congregations in the 21st Century* (Westminster John Knox Press)

"Given the challenges facing the leadership of the Church today, Paul Wilkes's book is an absolute must for every lay or clergy person hungry to revive a sleeping congregation."

—Dr. Bob Edgar, General Secretary, National Council of the Churches of Christ in the U.S.A.; former Congressman from Pennsylvania

Excellent ✦

✦ Protestant

Congregations

The Guide to
Best Places and Practices

Paul Wilkes

Westminster John Knox Press
LOUISVILLE • LONDON

Book and cover design by Cynthia Dunne

First edition
Published by Westminster John Knox Press
Louisville, Kentucky

This book is printed on acid-free paper that meets the American National Standards Institute Z39.48 standard. ∞

PRINTED IN THE UNITED STATES OF AMERICA

01 02 03 04 05 06 07 08 09 10—10 9 8 7 6 5 4 3 2

Library of Congress Cataloging-in-Publication Data
Wilkes, Paul, 1938–
    Excellent Protestant congregations: the guide to best places and practices / Paul Wilkes.
        p. cm.
    ISBN 0-664-22329-X (pbk.)
    1. Protestant churches—United States—Case studies. 2. Pastoral theology—United States—Case studies. I. Title.

    BX4805.3.W55   2001
    280'.4'0973—dc21   00-053455

Contents

Introduction ix

1. Lutheran Ministries of Southwest Oklahoma ✦ 1

Lone Wolf, Oklahoma

St. John's is the hub for Lutheran Ministries of Southwest Oklahoma. There may be only an auto parts store and a cafe on the otherwise boarded-up Main Street in Lone Wolf, but this dynamic, transforming church has a myriad of activities for every age group. Innovative work is being done across denominational lines.

2. Seekers Church ✦ 21

Washington, D.C.

Gordon Cosby and the Church of the Saviour are well known, but **Seekers** represents the second generation of this ministry, which is at work in a tough neighborhood in Washington, D.C. The power of a small number of committed, covenanted members whose small churches are each focused on a specific mission is explored.

3. MountainTop Community Church ✦ 39

Birmingham, Alabama

MountainTop is a second-generation Willow Creek–type, seeker-sensitive church. This is a growing church where innovative Christian education, dramas, "life issues" preaching, and Acts 2 governance are key.

4. All Saints Episcopal Church ✦ 57

Worcester, Massachusetts

All Saints is an old-line church that has reached out to its changing neighborhood. Black and white, poor and middle class worship together here, where great social outreach is a hallmark. When a murder happens on these mean streets, parishioners reconsecrate the ground with an on-site service. A labyrinth brings spiritual insights.

5. Riverside Baptist Church ✦ 7 1

Denver, Colorado

Riverside is an exciting multicultural church that addresses specific congregations, including a service for bikers! Here is niche evangelizing at its best, plus the founding of many satellite churches and innovative work to teach people how to evangelize in everyday life.

6. First United Methodist Church ✦ 8 9

Santa Monica, California

First United Methodist's first senior woman pastor has implemented a new style of lay-driven leadership that has given the 125-year-old church new life. Along with an outstanding music program and relevant, inspiring preaching, the church also has a strong presence in the community through its building of housing for homeless families and affordable apartments for the elderly.

7. Chinese Christian Union Church ✦ 1 O7

Chicago, Illinois

Set in Chinatown, **Chinese Christian Union Church** ministers to recent immigrants from mainland China and Taiwan, as well as to ABCs (American-Born Chinese), with a rich array of programs and approaches. Courses in the English language, citizenship, and an excellent bookstore— along with social events—attract new congregants.

8. Full Gospel Church of God in Christ ✦ 123

New Orleans, Louisiana

Full Gospel, an African American tithing church, gives hope in a tough inner-city neighborhood of New Orleans. Programs educate the entire person, but from a religious perspective. Community outreach and mentoring of young men is strong here.

9. Warehouse 242 ✦ 139

Charlotte, North Carolina

Warehouse 242 is a thriving, dynamic Gen-X church, less than a year old, but drawing growing numbers of hard-to-reach postmodern people. Its C.pak small groups attract non-Christians and encourage members to take religious beliefs into their work and personal lives. The transformation of the entire city is their mission.

Final Thoughts 157

Common Traits of Excellent Congregations 163

Points of Excellence Index 173

Index of Excellent Congregations 197

Introduction

This look at excellent Protestant congregations began, strangely enough, in a Catholic parish in New Jersey. I had been invited to give a series of talks at the Church of the Presentation in Upper Saddle River and, during the three days I spent there, found myself simply amazed with the vitality of the place, the obvious enjoyment people had in being part of the parish, the stories of transformation that I heard, of outreach, inreach. It was only when I returned to my home parish that the contrast struck me. I did not have such a place for my family and myself.

But if that wonderful, spirit-filled place in New Jersey existed, I was sure it was not the only example of excellent parish life. I wanted to find others and tell their stories. Through the generosity of a Lilly Endowment grant, I began the Parish/Congregation Study, whose object was to find not only excellent Catholic parishes but also excellent Protestant congregations. For the first volume of this study, I found some three hundred excellent parishes and profiled eight of them in *Excellent Catholic Parishes: The Guide to Best Places and Practices.*

I quickly realized that the search for excellent Protestant congregations would be a more complex assignment because of the many expressions of belief within the churches of the Reformation. But my object was no different. So, with the help of two expert researchers, Marty Minchin and Melanie Bruce, the Parish/Congregation Study went in search of excellence—local Protestant church excellence.

We set up criteria for these excellent congregations and cast a wide net, asking those in congregational renewal, those who studied church life, denominational and nondenominational experts, religion reporters, and those who addressed certain constituencies (Asian or African American, rural, inner-city, for example). But there was something more that we were looking for, something that in certain ways is less quantifiable yet is readily apparent when experienced.

Quite honestly, we were looking for congregations that had what the writer Flannery O'Connor called "a habit of being": congregations with a soul. We were looking for churches that impacted the lives of their people and were making a difference in their communities, local churches that were beacons of hope and guidance and examples of what it really means to be a practicing Christian today. Age, location, status, affiliation to a larger body or lack of it were not the issues. That "habit of being," wherever it could be found and however it was manifested, was.

For, while the so-called mainline churches have seen a decline both in their numbers and in denominational loyalty over the past two or three decades, this has been countered by an equally dramatic rise of both unaffiliated churches and a broad-based burgeoning of interest in spirituality. The desire for a spiritual connection with God seems as strong (or even stronger) as it ever has been in a nation that has seen so much material success yet looks for a deeper meaning to life. And the local church is still the place where the overwhelming majority of people find spiritual sustenance and support.

Indeed, the days are waning in which a denominational affiliation can reliably be counted upon to be both part of a person's description of one's self and a birthright that can be handed down to his or her children. But those are institutional issues, and if there was an advantage to the Parish/ Congregation Study, it was that I and the two researchers were not representatives of an institution and had no ideology to promote or hierarchy to please. In other words, we were not *of* the church; but we could be *in* the churches.

As with the book on Catholic parishes, this book is not about theory—or trends or statistics—but about practice, practical application. It is meant to be a sort of survival guide for pastors and church leaders. For as we sought excellence, we sought *reproducible* excellence. What we would look for in these churches would be approaches and programs that could be replicated in other places.

And for those seeking a home for their souls, we wanted to provide—if we might be so bold—a sort of Protestant Michelin Guide of excellent churches throughout America that are worthy homes for the spirit. We were certainly aware that we would not find all of the excellent Protestant congregations in America, but we wanted to find a good number of them. Of the three hundred congregations that we eventually found, nine of them are profiled. We have attempted to present a diverse group of churches from every part of the country. They do not look alike, and their approaches are quite different.

The pastors, staff, and lay people in these churches are not magicians of some kind; they do not possess secrets inaccessible to the rest of us. That is why they are worthy of being known and of serving as models for those local churches brave enough to really believe that God is with them—and will allow him to work in their midst.

For each church I have noted three "Points of Excellence," approaches that the church does especially well. Because we discovered so many points of excellence, the overflow of excellent approaches continues on page 173. Also, while there are pictures throughout the book, you may want to go to our web site, www.pastoralsummit.org, for more pictures and information about these wonderful churches.

Lutheran Ministries of Southwest Oklahoma

P.O. Box 368

Lone Wolf, OK 73655

580-846-5459

www.lutheranok.com

✦   POINTS OF EXCELLENCE   ✦

1. Refreshing the liturgy: the beginning of church renewal

2. "Growth Council": creative structures outside usual congregational governance

3. Partnership with other small churches and across denominational lines while keeping Lutheran identity

With the 1990 Census approaching, the people of Lone Wolf, Oklahoma, were understandably pleased that a new Lutheran pastor and his wife were coming to town. After all, this once-prosperous farming town 135 miles southwest of Oklahoma City had seen many leave and virtually no one come to stay for years. All new faces were welcome, perhaps signs that there could be a brighter future.

But unbeknownst to them, Bill Geis, the new pastor of St. John's Lutheran Church, was bringing more baggage than he had stuffed into his 1973 AMC Hornet. A middling seminary student at Concordia Seminary in St. Louis who had skipped more classes than he cared to admit, he was—on one hand—facing his assignment with a certain resignation. It was the obligatory first assignment to a small, rural church, and he had secretly vowed to himself that if he could last three years in this (using the term advisedly) godforsaken part of southwest Oklahoma, he would consider it an accomplishment.

But there was something else in twenty-seven-year-old Bill Geis's makeup, a counterbalance to that wariness. There was a fervor, an excitement. As conflicted a soul as he was, Bill Geis wanted to make a difference. He wanted to enliven the faith of people he knew felt the world had left them behind. He had felt that way himself at times. More than knowing only the tenets of their faith, he wanted his small flock to take their beliefs and faith into their lives. He wanted to bring hope to a place that was clearly down on itself.

If today's Main Street in Lone Wolf is any measure of the success of Bill Geis's efforts, he would be judged an utter failure. For Main Street—a reduced-speed-limit swath of Highway 9 that runs between Norman to the east and Texas to the west—is little more than a series of closed, abandoned stores. A few blank-faced, obviously unsold, grave markers stare out forlornly from Bob Richardson's yard, boarded-up buildings abound, and the charred shell of what used to be the state motor vehicle registry is testimony to both youthful mischievousness and deadening rural ennui. Only the Coyote Grill and Wegner's Auto Parts still struggle for survival. A huge orange water tower with the town's faded name and a towering, six-silo grain elevator speak of better, but bygone, days.

And, over at the high school, four girls got pregnant last year, 80 percent of the school kids qualify for school lunches, and teenagers with brown paper bags hardly concealing where they think easy pleasure will come from are still a common sight.

But if it would be possible, instead, to look beneath some of these externals and to get a picture of the Main Street of people's souls, not only in Lone Wolf, but in the surrounding towns, it would be another story all together. Bill Geis has wrought a somewhat miraculous transformation. Hope indeed has returned to Lone Wolf. People now say where they come from, proudly, not with heads hung low. Cooperation, not only among various denominations but also among towns, has blossomed. Faith is alive, and it is lived.

This is even stranger to comprehend when we consider the religious and cultural ethos of this part of the country. When Bill Geis and his wife, Sandi, came to town, Lutherans had a somewhat unenviable reputation—at least for avowed followers of Christ. There was an elitist air to them, some non-Lutherans thought; they were arrogant people who kept to themselves, seemed to look down on others and to do better than most—almost like Jews were sometimes regarded in Christian places. The previous Lutheran pastor had never deigned to share even a baccalaureate stage with other ministers for high school graduations, and he steered clear of the local ministerial alliance. Non-Lutherans would equally

Jesus Club members

never think to so much as set foot inside a Lutheran church, as they knew they would not be welcome. Tiny Christian churches fought for turf, even as they continued to lose members and their ability to serve the ones who were left.

"It was clear to me this was not about theology; this was about relationships," Bill says early one morning as we wait for his men's Bible study group to gather. "I wanted to get into their lives; I wanted to demythologize the ministry. I wanted to convince them that we are all human, we all lose hope, we all wonder if we can make it. I wanted them to know that we were in this together—as human beings." So Bill didn't preach Lutheran triumphalism or split doctrinal hairs. He set out to meet the people with whom he would spend the next three years.

Feeling much like a foreigner in the community—in fact, rural ministry has been likened to missionary work in an overseas country—Bill spent his first few months getting to know people. "I didn't have a clue about living in a rural community, and since I was so ignorant, I had to learn from the people. I just hung around. I did chores on a farm. I taught classes at the high school. I sat in coffee shops. I knew about computers and had been a financial consultant, so I taught classes for farmers to help manage their accounts." As Bill Geis talks, his early innocence and these memories seem so precious to him. He has sandy hair, perhaps a pound or two that he might not need, and a sweet, rounded face that welcomes you in, the kind of face you can get lost in, a face that accepts and doesn't demand.

"I thought that if anyone was going to change this town, it was these people. I thought that Christians should have the opportunity to repair the social structures. People had stopped dreaming. They had to be told they could dream again. And that their dreams could come true."

But all his passion and good intentions did not immediately bring people around. Pessimism was long-standing and profound in rural Oklahoma. "One fellow said, 'Don't get too excited and start getting things going, because you're going to be our last pastor,'" Bill Geis recalls, as the inevitable closing of the church was being forecast. There were three funerals in the first six weeks he was there, the grief for the deceased and their dying church interwoven.

But the situation that Bill looks back upon as the defining event of his first few years of ministry occurred when the town found out that Philip Tepe, a teenage hemophiliac in the church, had full-blown AIDS. He had contracted the disease through blood transfusions throughout his childhood, and the family had kept it a secret for years at the doctors' advice, because at that time AIDS was associated primarily with homosexuals and drug users. "People thought that good Christian people didn't get AIDS," says Dorecia Tepe, Philip's mother, who still lives in Lone Wolf with her husband, Jimmy. "If you got AIDS it was because you deserved it. It was really something that I don't think our community ever thought about deeper than that."

The community was in an uproar because Philip played on the basketball team, which had won the division championship that year only because so many other teams forfeited their games against Philip's team. *Sports Illustrated* had even run a short article about the conflict. Sports are a key part of small-town life, but Bill Geis took a public stand against the ignorance of some of the community and stood by the family, even as other local pastors told him that he should advise the family to remove Philip from the basketball team for the safety of the other players. Privately, throughout the ordeal, Bill frequently prayed with the family and visited Philip in the hospital in Oklahoma City, a two-hour drive from Lone Wolf. "I know it was tough on Bill too, but our pastor was right there when we needed him," says Dorecia. "People might have disagreed with him, but they could see what kind of man he was." Philip Tepe died in 1994, and Bill Geis buried him with dignity and pride.

Bill had already begun to change worship, which he considered the crucial first step. Frustrated with the lack of an easy way to implement new ideas, he created what he called a "Growth Council." A new spirit was being born just as he received a call to be the pastor at a young, upbeat, six-hundred-member church in New Jersey. It was, to many Lutheran ministers, a "dream church," and almost the exact opposite of Lone Wolf. "It really was a spiritual experience," Bill says of the call, one of seven he has received while at Lone Wolf. "It was exciting for a young person like me. But I was just beginning to see what had to be done. I couldn't leave now. I said to myself, 'I'm staying here.'"

Of the 6,200 congregations in the Missouri Synod of the Lutheran Church—of which Bill Geis is a member—there are usually some 1,000 pastoral vacancies. Seminaries are not producing pastors quickly enough, so there is continual

✦ 1. REFRESHING THE LITURGY: THE BEGINNING OF CHURCH RENEWAL ✦

Changing the worship service was Bill Geis's first step in his attempt to transform the culture of a town. "This is where we had to start, because without a service that really binds people together and sends them out with a specific message and with courage, you can't do a thing," he says. He changed, as he says, "music that was too much thirteenth-century Gregorian chant to something that was more akin to nineteenth-century gospel." He took old melodies and wrote new lyrics and printed them in the bulletin. He has also built a small stage area around the altar so the choir can be brought to the front of the church and skits can dramatize the gospel message. While keeping the elements of a traditional Lutheran service, he constantly restructures it. Instead of the traditional Lutheran confession, Pastor Geis will write a specific one, corresponding to the day's scripture. For instance, speaking of Christ's heart: "When I look at your Heart for the lost, I am ashamed. Yes I have heart for some, however there are others." And then the absolution: "Receive the power of God: he forgives you . . . may the power of this heavenly affirmation stir up the kind potency that God desires for you around the lost people he is pursuing."

turnover, especially in the smaller churches. Bill Geis was going against the expected ministerial career trajectory.

By now his vision had reached beyond St. John's Lutheran in Lone Wolf to the Lutheran churches in the neighboring towns of Altus and Elk City, which had recently lost their

✦ 2. "GROWTH COUNCIL": CREATIVE STRUCTURES OUTSIDE USUAL CONGREGATIONAL GOVERNANCE ✦

While not tampering with the traditional forms of Lutheran Church governance, Bill Geis simply blazed a parallel path for his parish. "Governance wasn't creative; we needed to be creative," he says, "so I started what we called the 'Growth Council.' Anyone could be in it, could drop in or drop out. No elections, no officers. After all, some of the best suggestions you hear about are in the parking lot or the coffee shop. We just provided a way to bring that into the church." The Growth Council meets at least once a month. No idea is too bizarre; no formal presentation has to be made. It is the forum for all church members to have their say. "And from it, leaders emerged to take charge. Not necessarily formally elected, but they just wanted to carry out what they or some-one else suggested."

pastors and could not afford new ones—if pastors could even be found. In rural areas, the nationwide pastor shortage is even more acute, and pastors, especially good pastors, are hard to come by. While waiting for a permanent pastor, rural churches can languish for years under interim pastors or a shared pastor. And when many pastors do take rural assign-ments, often they are so geographically isolated that working alone quickly burns them out.

Directly confronting the disconnection and stolid individ-ualism in both the religious and secular communities that he had experienced, Bill got the idea of *partnership*. Taking the idea from the business community, in which KFC now some-times shares a building with Taco Bell and McDonald's mar-kets movies with its food, he realized that the one way to counter both the churches' and the communities' problems would be to work together. He now envisioned his parish as six counties; 4,500 square miles; and 80,000 people. His would not be a dual parish, which many denominations have tried and which involves two churches sharing a pastor, but a system where churches would keep their own identity and share their pastor *and* their resources. The churches would not compete, instead focusing their combined resources wherever they were most needed. While it would be difficult —and pastoral burnout would loom if he were not careful— Bill Geis gave it a try.

Because the three communities are so different—Altus, a town of 23,000, is centered around an Air Force base, and Elk City, with a population of about 9,000, is more affluent, a town that grew rich in the 1980s oil boom—and are at least thirty miles apart from one another, Bill Geis knew that con-solidating the congregations was not a good solution. For example, in Elk City, the four or five families that form the backbone of the church didn't want to close the church, but they didn't think merging with another congregation would be for the best either. "Uprooting people out of a community seems kind of backward," Bill agrees one day over lunch with Nan Buie and Cindi Scheuerman, members of Christ Lutheran Church in Elk City. "We have a building in Elk City that's paid for and some people who couldn't drive to another church," Nan says. "For me, I want my kids to be raised in this church. We asked, 'Does God want this church to close?' The answer we always heard was no."

Bill Geis continued to refine his idea of a partnership from watching how city and rural hospitals have teamed up to offer

✦ 3. PARTNERSHIP WITH OTHER SMALL CHURCHES AND ACROSS DENOMINATIONAL LINES WHILE KEEPING DENOMINATIONAL IDENTITY ✦

In Lone Wolf and the surrounding towns, various Protestant churches already had worked together on Thanksgiving baskets for the needy and a joint Christmas program, but, as Bill Geis says, "that was all on the surface. We hadn't really entrusted our people to each other; we were very territorial." The effort that broke through that surface was the unification of all the tiny youth programs in Lone Wolf. Disciples of Christ, Methodist, Baptist, and Lutheran teens now have a program with enough kids to create a critical mass and allow for substantial programming. "We have to get over the thought of another church 'taking over,' we have to let go, trust and allow the leadership to emerge from whatever denomination can do it best," Pastor Bill Geis says. "It may be our idea, but we do not have to be the leaders." Now partnership is so common in Lutheran Ministries of Southwest Oklahoma that it is often the first choice, rather than a default position.

better health care to rural areas. "People pick and choose their faith today, so I said, 'Let's offer them a menu.' If you capitalize on your gifts, you can cross-promote your ministry. Everyone doesn't have to do open-heart surgery; better to have one place that does it well. It's also taking the idea of how the Internet is evolving, where new links are forming every day. We can rebuild the infrastructure by creating a web of relational links. Yes, we will keep our distinctive Lutheran ways, but we are not talking about denominational issues, we're talking about people issues, meeting people's needs, providing ways for people who are churched and unchurched, Lutheran and non-Lutheran to get together. And not just me —the people would have to do it. Having a team of workers is better than one lone ranger trying to save the world."

Again, Bill Geis's grand plan was not always welcomed. He was called Satan, a liberal, a New Age evil prophet who was not vigilant enough in guarding access to the Eucharist. Printing words to songs in the bulletin instead of using the venerable hymnbook was akin to apostasy. In one church, the church treasurer curtly handed over both the books and a resignation. But Bill Geis knew he was on to something, and even with small—but spirited—dissent, he went on.

While it took several years to fully catch on, the partnership between the Lutheran churches in Lone Wolf, Altus, and Elk City slowly began to bear fruit. "I think people had to digest it and think about it, and more and more people saw that it was the future," says Ronald Boelte, Bill's assisant pastor. As Bill says, his parishioners have become "bloodhounds for opportunities to partner," and that has resulted in combined youth groups and other programs across denominational lines and a combined budget for the three Lutheran churches.

The partnership is also forging connections between people who would have never known of one another without the partnership. "My dream is that I want people to have a bigger picture of what the body of Christ is," Bill told Parish/ Congregation Study researcher Marty Minchin during her visit to Lone Wolf. And while the first seeds of that are the simple, small changes that seem minor on their own, they are contributing to an awakening of hope and renewal within people in all three congregations. For example, the monthly Festive Hope service in Lone Wolf, where all of the congregations gather for an hour and a half of worship and prayer and a potluck snack afterward, is not like a junior high dance with Lone Wolfers on one side and Altus congregants on the other. Both casseroles and prayers soar over what were once unbreachable barriers between towns and people.

A tragic death proved a milestone for the partnership in Southwest Oklahoma. After her son Kit was killed in an automobile accident, Nickie Straub asked Bill that her son's funeral be a sign of unity among the churches. "If something good can come of this, if we can learn something about cooperation," she said, "it would be a fitting memorial to Kit." The funeral was exactly that, with all the local ministers officiating, standing together as a town shared its sorrow, denominational affiliation put aside.

Bill Geis's dreams continue to run deeper than simply acquainting the congregations and ministers with each other. No one realizes more than he that pastoring three rural churches is a taxing job for one person. Sunday mornings, for example, can literally be a race against time, as he will preach the 8:30 A.M. service in Altus, then drive seventy-five miles to Elk City, arriving just in time to preach at their 10:30 A.M. service. In a typical month, he can log four thousand miles on the family car. He knows such a pace will wear him down eventually, so he has hopes of changing the congregations' whole view of the pastorship. He wants lay people to become leaders and to take more responsibility for both church duties and caring for the people. "We are grinding away at the idea that the pastor is the only important person," he says with his usual infectious enthusiasm. "Fifty, I want to have fifty lay leaders who have personal ownership of the ministry."

And while he hasn't yet spawned fifty assistant lay pastors, people are slowly accepting and even embracing the idea. Andy Anderson at Faith Lutheran in Altus has taken on new

Tuesday morning Bible study

responsibilities in the church. "I think everybody's willing to do more than just their little share," he says at a weekly meeting of representatives from each congregation where issues and decisions involving the partnership are discussed. "I used to go to church now and then and that was it. Now instead of being onlookers like we used to be, we're involved. It makes you feel like you have a little worth in your life. It makes you feel a little better."

John Dee Butchee heads up a well-attended men's Bible study on Tuesday mornings, and Melissa Hunter, a seventeen-year-old high school senior whom Pastor Geis said was once impossibly shy, is a principal singer during the worship. Although she stares down at her microphone during some of the songs, Pastor Geis knows that getting up in front of the church is a huge accomplishment. At Jesus Club, the Wednesday after-school program for Lone Wolf School students, Melissa leads children's games and prayer time. "We've learned that other people have gifts," Kim Bryant, from Altus, says. "Pastor Geis doesn't have to be there to give his blessing on everything to make it a success."

Norma Wegner, who never considered herself a spiritual leader, is a member of a prayer group, that has had a 100 percent success rate of people they've prayed for to return to church. Granted, not all of them stayed, but they at least passed through the church doors. Virginia Robison, who left St. John's in 1988 for a local Methodist church that had more activities for children, is a "worked on" person who stayed, although she doesn't seem aware that she has been the object of many church members' prayers for months. Katey, her twelve-year-old daughter, who was unhappy at the church they were attending, loves St. John's so much that she has voluntarily skipped cheerleading practice to attend confirmation class. Virginia's older daughter, who's seventeen, has made friends with Melissa Hunter and another teenage girl at the church and has come through a tough stretch on her road to adulthood because of their support. Stan, Virginia's husband, who had stopped going to church a few years ago, now attends church and Sunday school at St. John's.

"It's like coming back home," says Virginia, a quiet, thoughtful woman in her mid-thirties, whose deep faith is evident. "It's different now. We just kept coming back." Her return to Lone Wolf has resulted in some radical changes in her own life. After reading the weekly devotions that Bill writes and prints in the church bulletin, Virginia found the inspiration to quit a difficult job as the activities director at a senior center before she had another job lined up. "I told our pastor I felt like he wrote those words just for me."

But perhaps the most dramatic example of Lone Wolf's new lay leadership is Ronald Boelte, who grew up on a farm outside of town. A soft-spoken man with neatly combed black hair and glasses, Ronald looks like he would be much more comfortable on a tractor than in a pulpit. And in truth, he once was. But there was always something nagging at him as he was growing up. "I always felt that God was maybe calling me to greater things, but I didn't know what. It's taken quite a few years to convince me it was ministry." Bill suggested that he enroll in a lay ministry program, and for five years Ronald drove an hour and a half once a month to attend eight hours of classes.

And now at a Sunday service at Faith Lutheran in Altus, it is Bill Geis who sits with the congregation while Ronald, wearing the white pastor's robes, leads the service and delivers the sermon. His hands shake slightly while he teaches a lesson on forgiveness, using a bag of pennies as an illustration of God's unlimited mercy, but his delivery is clear and his sermon obviously well thought out. "Preaching. That's one of those things that I thought I'd never do," Ronald says over lunch at the Coyote Grill on one of the days he works as a farmer. "I waited until my senior year in college to take speech because I didn't want to get up in front of people." But, as he and most congregants—who have encouraged Ronald through his difficult and awkward first year of preaching—would agree, he's made vast improvements. "A year ago you could have blinked at me during a sermon and I would have forgotten everything."

"I think he's critical to the new way of ministry," Bill Geis says. "He's a pioneer because by his professional involvement with our staff and his leadership he's paved the way for future lay leaders to be raised up. He's a person of impeccable integrity, and we needed someone like him to lead this whole thing. It's not so much what he does as how he changes people's perceptions."

While Bill has prodded some church members into leadership, he has nudged others into community involvement. He and Sandi have set the example, hosting a lavish community Easter cantata every year that includes a choir of people from all Lone Wolf churches, no small feat considering that Lone Wolf School has traditionally not had a music program and few in the town's churches have had any formal musical training. Church members rave about the program, and stories, such as the one about Sandi's staying up all night before the cantata to decorate the stage with flowers that community members had dropped off the day before, have become legendary. Sandi also ran for the school board—on a controversial platform of putting more emphasis on education and less on sports—and although she narrowly lost, it prompted an examination of a town's priorities.

But even more so than making themselves known in the community, Bill, Sandi, and the church's members realize that to grow, they have to reach unchurched people in their communities. In Altus, the church staff did some research and learned that other churches' Mother's Day Out programs had waiting lists. So they started their own at Faith Lutheran—this, in a church that once had a horrible reputation in the community after several ugly splits over issues such as who was allowed to take Communion at the Sunday service. "Faith Lutheran was dying," says Mona Hunter, the feisty, outspoken director of children's ministries for the churches. "We feel strongly that there needs to be a Lutheran presence here. This program provides a way for the community to get to know who we are."

The situation is much different in Lone Wolf, where the church has an amicable relationship with the community, but the problems with the town's children are more serious. Students often reek of marijuana, elementary-age children are having sex, and many teenagers have drinking problems. Their home lives are often disjointed—many have parents who are divorced and are living with a boyfriend or girlfriend; others have several siblings who each have a different father. In response, St. John's started Jesus Club, a holistic after-school program on Wednesday afternoons. "The Jesus

Club kids don't go to church anywhere else," Bill says. "These are unchurched kids with a lot of behavioral problems. This ministry tends to attract more misfits than high achievers, which we're pretty proud of, actually."

Mona also leads a BYOB (Bring Your Own Bible) for youth from all three Lutheran churches. "We used shock value to get the kids to stop and look," Mona says of the group's questionable name. Between eight and ten attend the Bible study, where they still pray for football and baseball victories, but where conversations with God are transforming the group. "There's an openness to talk about God that wasn't there before," she says. "And we've been told by the schools that it does make a difference in some of the more hard to handle kids."

Bill Geis quickly learned that in rural areas, aside from economic issues, people are often also isolated and unnecessarily independent. "That means that they don't share their problems, don't get too involved in others' lives, and most certainly don't ask anyone else to help them," he says. "But, of course the gospel is all about sharing each other's burdens, of lending a hand. People just need to be shown a way that it can be done."

On the Tuesday morning I am in Lone Wolf, as the members of the men's Bible study group wander into the well-used activity room near the 7 A.M. meeting time, it is not hard to see that these are plain speaking, hard working, independent men—the kind who have farmed this land for generations. Dressed in bib overalls and flannel shirts, they are on their way to work; but this is obviously an important first stop. One describes his former prayer life as "so much hot air going up a chimney" and admits to the general deadness of his spirituality before he came to this group. "Hey, without getting together with you guys, my week isn't complete," he says. Others talk of finally knowing Lutheran men in outlying towns and of a new sense of fellowship and pride. "We can pray for each other and that's what makes us strong." Still another man talked of his personal goal: to get a friend back to church. His technique is simple: He makes it a point to stop at his shop every week and talk for a half hour or so, often about church, but sometimes the subject never comes up. "I'm going to get him," he says with a confident smile.

The rhythms of the church year and the messages of the scripture they hear both in the pews and around tables with a tall thermos of coffee and sausage and egg biscuits are now woven into the very fabric of these Oklahoma towns. And as Norma Wegner, who's been a member of St. John's for almost fifty years, says, "Since Pastor Geis came, we've become . . . well . . . we've become a hugging church." Wayne Schreiner, a farmer who has been faithfully involved in the church for fifty years, says, "I turn to God a lot more than I used to. I used to be much more self-reliant." Through painstaking pastoral work—one person, one crisis, one funeral, one baptism, one encouragement at a time—Bill Geis has profoundly changed not only the spiritual lives of many people but also the culture of a town. Amid what some might call ample reason for despair, he has instilled in his people a dynamic faith in God and taught them that with God, they can look beyond their despair and dream great dreams. When Bill Geis talks about fifty lay leaders and ten thousand people coming to church as if it were just over the next rise in the road, his people find their own dreams equally possible.

All this from a seemingly classic underachiever, a man who would drop his wife off at work en route to the seminary and, instead of going to classes, drive hundreds of miles to pass the time and then pick up his wife. (When she would ask him how his day at seminary was, he would always tell her, "Fine.") From a pastor who doesn't hide his emotions, cries easily, and won't hide the fact that his feelings are hurt. He's disorganized, not quite charismatic in the classic sense, and has a difficult time with rejection—hardly the hallmarks of a successful pastor, yet his congregations adore him, although not all of them are exactly sure why. "If people are to trust you, you have to be open with them, honest about your own life," he says.

"For some reason or other, he's just able to touch everybody," says Norma Wegner. "I don't even know an adjective to describe him," says Sarah Schreiner, another longtime member who has seen many a pastor come and go. "He is so gracious, and no matter what anybody does to him, he loves them back. He won our hearts from the time he came."

At Concordia Seminary a little over a decade ago, few probably thought that Bill Geis would someday be considered a cutting-edge pastor, one constantly being offered bigger and more prestigious churches. But by inserting himself not only into the lives of his people, but also into the very nature and culture of Lone Wolf and the surrounding towns, he has shown what rural ministry can be. Humble in his manner yet incredibly audacious in his dreams, Bill Geis put himself and God on the line.

They both—the folks out this way would agree—measured up.

Seekers Church

278 Carroll Street NW
Washington, D.C. 20012
202-829-9882
www.seekerschurch.org

✦ POINTS OF EXCELLENCE ✦

1. Committed and covenanted

2. Creativity in worship

3. Educating every lay member

The accidental tourist traveling through the Adams-Morgan district in Washington, D.C., is readily exposed to the outward face of this fascinating, complex neighborhood. There is a smorgasbord of ethnic restaurants and sidewalk vendors and a mix of expensive housing and slum dwellings, for this is one of those neighborhoods benignly termed "transitional," where the homeless share the narrow, bustling sidewalks with fast-walking Gen Xers on their way to Capitol Hill jobs.

As might be expected, the soul of Adams-Morgan is not so apparent.

Those who know this neighborhood might say that the soul of Adams-Morgan resides behind a collection of storefronts and buildings little different in outward appearance from those that stand to their left and right. There are no great church buildings, no huge signs, very little proclaiming that more than fifty years ago a tiny group of people—three, in fact—with no institutional affiliation, backing, or support, and no clergy, set about to transform Adams-Morgan.

Developers of a sort, they cast their lot among society's poor, to turn these streets into a new Jerusalem, a city upon a hill. For these buildings and storefronts—which call no attention to themselves—and the people within them, are part of a remarkable church, fired with a vision at once ancient and revolutionary. It was originally called the Church of the Saviour and, while other churches might aspire to greater numbers, it has always concentrated on a deeper, covenanted commitment. There has never been any actual church structure. It still thrives on smallness. In fact, in 1976 when the Church of the Saviour reached some 140 members —barely a modest-sized congregation—it was disbanded, its members free to form new communities that would allow them to better address what they would discern were the pressing needs around them.

One of the nine "churches" that eventually formed is called Seekers, and its members chose child advocacy as their mission focus. Some of them are lawyers who work in child advocacy for Housing and Urban Development (HUD) or the Defense Department, and others work for grassroots development in South America. Still others operate Hope

✦ 1. COMMITTED AND COVENANTED ✦

The small churches that have sprung from the Church of the Saviour continue a commitment to smallness. While this is seemingly the opposite of logical church growth strategy, it ensures that every member is truly a minister. Members serve as the governing body of the church, taking on the jobs performed by deacons, elders, and pastors in traditional churches. Becoming a core member is essentially an ordination—prospective members are required to take in-depth classes on Christian belief and doctrine and to take on administrative and sacramental duties in the church. "Our commitment is to care about the whole church," says Marjory Bankson of Seekers Church.

The heart of that commitment is in its mission groups, a requirement of membership. This is where true community is fostered, where members not only band together toward common service and goals, but also where they form deep friendships, pray for one another, and help one another through life's struggles. Each weekly meeting, where attendance is mandatory except under exceptional circumstances, involves worship, silence, sharing, prayer, and work on that group's mission, which could be anything from teaching in Seekers' School of Christian Living to looking for a new location for the church. When the mission is considered completed, the group will disband and reformulate around another mission.

and a Home, a seventeen-unit building that houses poor families with children and helps them become self-sufficient.

Celebration Circle mission group

Others create innovative liturgies that will involve children in their Sunday service. Marjory Bankson, one of its current twenty-four members, teaches in the Seekers Christian Leadership School, where people can take courses ranging from Christian ethics to liturgical clowning. "We try to keep our groups—we call them mission groups, and they can comprise from three to as many as ten or twelve people—focused on gifts and calls: a person's abilities and the actual need that has presented itself," she says. "We pray a lot and discuss a lot over this, but it is pretty simple, actually. We need to help mothers and kids with a place to thrive; we need to change public policy; we need to educate our own children about what it means to live out the gospel mandate."

"We always look to the 'edges,'" says Sonya Dyer, a cofounder of Seekers. "What can we do that nobody else is doing and is screaming out to happen?" Marjory Bankson adds the crucial element: "And we want what we do to also change us. What we do needs to be like sandpaper on our souls."

Marjory and Sonya, two attractive gray-haired women whose chronological ages are rendered irrelevant by their vibrancy, represent a second generation of Church of the Saviour leadership who have taken on the clear, simple—but demanding—vision of Church of the Saviour's founder, Gordon Cosby. In the more than fifty years of its existence, Church of the Saviour has provided a beacon of hope and practical help in this neighborhood, sounded a call for social justice in the seats of government, and rippled across the country to churches who see this as an example of what an Acts 2 church can be.

The inner-city work of the Church of the Saviour communities is by no means random—members are not recruited to work in a soup kitchen once a month or to collect canned food for the homeless. The process is much more deliberate in these intentional communities, beginning with the notion of God bringing a problem to the attention of one of their members. The person then prays and mulls over the idea within his or her small church group and eventually leads or takes part in a mission to address the problem. This idea of "call" is what the Church of the Saviour was built upon, as members over the years responded to ideas they believe the Holy Spirit implanted within them.

While this process may sound haphazard or even improbable, Adams-Morgan is a testament to amazing stories of people from Church of the Saviour who have answered God's call to work there. The Potter's House, between Sixteenth and Seventeenth Streets on Columbia Road NW, is the anchor of a string of ministries that Church of the Saviour progeny own and operate. The Potter's House was created as a coffeehouse where those earliest members of the Church of the Saviour could simply listen to the neighborhood. As they listened, they learned that affordable housing was virtually

✦ 2. CREATIVITY IN WORSHIP ✦

One defining characteristic of Seekers among its Church of the Saviour sister churches is its emphasis on creativity, which members believe is a manifestation of God's continuing work. Worship at Seekers is a creation of its members, who write the liturgy, make the altar decorations, and write or perform sermons and lessons. They much prefer to create things on their own than to buy them, which is part of what Marjory Bankson calls "living a handmade life." That, Marjory says, brings them closer to God. "We basically believe that God is not a static God, but we are part of an ongoing creation," she says. "We use images, as well as words, to express our faith. It gives us all a stake in the worship and it gives us a unique identity as a congregation."

Creation also provides an outlet for Seekers members whose day jobs don't allow for artistic expression. Peter Bankson, who his wife, Marjory, calls "a very creative man," is renowned at Seekers for turning things he finds in his basement into beautiful altar adornments. Other members of Celebration Circle, the Seekers group that oversees the church's liturgy, use their talents as poets to write liturgy. "They have fun, they play," Marjory says. "It's part of what the Sabbath is about—remembering God as creator." Seekers' liturgies are available at www.seekerschurch.org.

nonexistent, so a drug-infested building was purchased, rehabilitated, and now provides that safe haven for poor families and individuals.

When a doctor found a homeless man frozen to death in a phone booth where he had tried to find warmth from the cold, she was first outraged, then resolute that an infirmary was needed. The fact that she had no money to buy or renovate a building for such a project didn't faze her or other Church of the Saviour members.

About that time, a wealthy woman who had read about the Church of the Saviour decided to tithe her money to the church, although she had no idea how much money she had. While she totaled her assets, the doctor had architects draw up plans for a thirty-bed infirmary. The estimated cost to build the infirmary came to more than $2 million, just about the same amount as the wealthy woman's tithe.

Often, ministries that started when one person receives a call will continue to draw people into its work for years. Sally Holmes, a social worker and a new mother who is a fairly recent Seekers member, moved to Washington from Texas specifically to be part of this church. She met her husband, Paul, at Seekers, and found a family within the close-knit community. "Everybody else knew we were going to get married before we did," she says. She also found her dream job, working with A Hope and a Home. "It was a case of God leading me," she says.

As I walked the streets of Adams-Morgan with Ray McGovern, who works with the Servant Leadership School that has initiated thousands in Church of the Saviour ways, it was almost as if we were visiting so many Stations of the Cross—places of human suffering—that had been transformed by divine grace and human initiative through this church's work. Columbia Road Health Services is a clinic for the district's most vulnerable residents; Christ House, a thirty-four-bed medical recovery facility for the homeless;

Kairos House, home to thirty-seven chronically ill indigents; Good Shepherd Ministries, a beehive of education and recreation programs for children; Samaritan Inn, which provides crucial transitional living to help the homeless rebuild their lives, is staffed by yearlong volunteer "Innkeepers." In eight buildings dotted throughout the neighborhood, Jubilee Housing now provides 284 apartments, Jubilee Jobs provides employment for the poor, and Sarah's Circle is made up of thirty-four apartments for the elderly with limited means. McGovern, who is Catholic, does not belong to one of the small communities but sought the deeper commitment and support Church of the Saviour provides. "You start to volunteer in these places and it just sweeps you away. You don't want to do anything else."

As for the lack of formally sanctioned clergy within the Church of the Saviour, its members usually shrug, but not with indifference or arrogance. "There are many ways to live out one's faith," says Sonya Dyer. "This is ours. What we have found is that, given the opportunity, you can evoke lay leadership that can articulate a modern-day theology that is both engaged in the world and committed to the gospel." Each of the small churches actually ordains certain members who have completed the training that church requires. Some go on to become licensed so they can perform weddings and funerals. But ordination is in a sense peripheral; it is the commitment to the work of the church that brings and keeps people there. The ordained have no greater place or privilege.

The radical differences between these Church of the Saviour offspring and most conventional churches is what Gordon Cosby calls "integrity of membership." It might seem an elementary enough phrase, but when people choose membership, they commit to dividing their energy between the church's focus on the "inward" and "outward" journeys, which,

Gordon Cosby

when equally attended to, result in a balance between the time they spend cultivating their own relationships with God (the inward journey) and doing God's work in the world (the outward journey). While visitors are always welcome at liturgies and as volunteers, there is no room for halfheartedness if one chooses membership in this church.

"We hope that we are always welcoming to people who come to our services," says Marjory, "but we realize membership is not for everyone. This will always be a small movement. If a person really wants to make this kind of commitment, it will transform your life—but you have to be willing to have that life transformed."

During an era in which popular culture celebrates individualism, materialism, and personal achievement—even the "name it and claim it" brand of success-driven Christianity—Seekers and the other Church of the Saviour churches are moving in the opposite direction. While the members have not sold all their worldly possessions and do not share all things in common as written about in Acts 2, the members do tithe. But it is not merely to maintain their own church, rather to forward their mission. Some 50 percent of the Seekers $190,000 annual budget goes to outside child advocacy groups and agencies, but a Seekers member is always involved in them.

In some ways, what Seekers has to offer would, on first glance, appear to scare people off rather than attract them. That is partially reflected in the church's attendance statistics, a reversal of the typical church that has many more members on its rolls than show up for Sunday service. At Seekers, four times as many people come to services and participate in mission groups than are members. And, if they attend regularly but do not choose to commit, they are encouraged to find a church that better fits their needs. If they do commit, they must join a mission group, where many ask that they submit weekly written reports of what's going on in their lives to a spiritual companion, often called a "faithful friend." Marjory Bankson has been giving two single-paged sheets to the same man in her group for twelve years. "He told me he's never been more intimate with anybody he hasn't slept with," she jokes.

"But I think one of the main appeals in Church of the Saviour–type churches is that people find a sense of support for an alternative lifestyle to what our culture dishes out," Marjory says. When Seekers' members describe their church, they talk about it as being their "life," their "spiritual home," and their "family."

That way of life and the closeness it inevitably harbors is obvious at the Seekers' Sunday liturgy, held in an imposing three-story Victorian brownstone at 2025 Massachusetts Avenue on Embassy Row. On this summer Sunday, twenty-four committed members, their children, and about seventy-five visitors are present. These range from people here for the first time to those who have been coming for a while and may or may not be involved in a mission group. Announcements range from a group meeting at 1 P.M. after church to see the new Star Wars movie to an elderly woman telling everyone that she would be gone the next weekend because she would be attending a relative's wedding. While there is no roll call, those who will not be in church the next Sunday always announce the fact. This is not done out of guilt, but because this is a small, accountable, and covenanted community whose members genuinely care about one another. Visitors are welcomed and asked to tell something about themselves and what brought them there. When announcements are over, the relaxed atmosphere of the room transforms into soundless reverence when Peter Bankson, Marjory's husband and the day's liturgist, strikes a handheld bell. The group files into the parlor in silence to begin worship.

The theme for the liturgy is "Incendiary Grace," as the Sunday bulletins—each with a hole burned through the cover—immediately dramatize. Before this small group is an altar whose only permanent adornment, a flat wooden cross, is decorated with a cloth woven from bright red, yellow, and orange strips wrought from last year's Pentecost banners. From the ceiling, suspended on three long chains, hangs a brass pot containing a small fire, a cold-burning flame that Peter, who now works with area schools but is an MIT graduate, created in his kitchen.

One hallmark of Seekers Church is its emphasis on creativity, underscoring their belief that God is still at work and creation is an ongoing process that people can be involved in. That means any given Sunday could include carefully written prayers that sound more like poetry or liturgical clowning that retells a biblical story. Seekers, like the other Church of the Saviour churches, doesn't have a preacher; all members have the authority to compose and deliver sermons. "As long as you can see over the lectern, you can preach at Seekers," Peter Bankson says.

On this Sunday, the richly conceived service has a powerful call to worship: "We come together, walking barefoot toward flame." After periods of Quakerlike silence, a litany, hymns, and readings from the traditional lectionary, a children's play is performed rather than a sermon. In *The Time Portal,* Tobin,

Andrew, Samantha, April, Marian, Jennifer, Shoshanna, and Lauren travel back in time to allow twenty-first-century Seekers Church members to meet first-century Christians. Amazingly, the tenets of the early Christians are what is needed today: no more people enslaved, women treated equally, care for "widows and orphans"—this is exactly what Seekers hopes to do for poor and abused children and their families in Washington. As for governance: no bishops and group decisions are among the revelations from the time travelers. The kids in sneakers and T-shirts have passed through the time portal; robed biblical figures return to our day to see what Seekers Church is all about. The result is a series of powerful lessons not taught *to* children, but *by* children to the rest of the congregation.

It is the infectious Church of the Saviour spirit, its services to the poor, and intelligent liturgies such as this that have brought people to these tiny churches over the past five decades. In fact, Ken Burton used to drive 150 miles round-trip from Philadelphia every week until he simply gave up and moved to Washington. A married couple, both physicians from Atlanta, whom I met at the noon service that is held in the Festival Center chapel, had closed their practices and moved to be part of the Church of the Saviour ministries. "I think people come because they are hungering for a degree of spiritual understanding and a place to live it out," says Sonya Dyer. "Parents who come to Seekers want more than Sunday school for their kids."

But even after accepting membership in Seekers or another of the Church of the Saviour family of communities, individuals are aware that the group and the mission they signed on for may not last. While many traditional churches today are dying because older members refuse to let go of the way things have been done for years or of a church building that may be completely wrong for today's congregation but is full of memories, Seekers and these other intentional communities embrace and welcome change. They believe that God can issue more than one call to an individual or a congregation in a lifetime, thus, they are always willing to move on if something isn't working or has run its course. Gordon Cosby has often said that in his lifetime he has seen more ministries die than preachers born.

For instance, on a wall in the room within 2025 Massachusetts Avenue where Seekers meets, there is a map of Washington with pushpins marking the locations of several buildings the church is looking to buy. Why wouldn't it just buy this beautiful house, one of the birthplaces of the Church of the Saviour? Sentimentality aside, the grand building simply doesn't meet what Seekers has discerned as its needs. Instead, Seekers plans to make an offer on a building at 1101 Pennsylvania Avenue, a somewhat prosaic two-story printing house between Capitol Hill and several huge housing projects. This building has bay windows, which would work well for studio art space. They are also considering opening a coffeehouse/bookstore to attract the Capitol Hill workers who might participate in lunchtime policy discussions.

A look back to the founding of Church of the Saviour and the implosion that led to Seekers and other mission-driven communities provides a strange and haunting reminder that biblical truths, faith, and prayer really can move mountains. While he was in the Army during World War II, Gordon had seen too many church-raised soldiers show no grasp of how Christian doctrine related to their lives. So he and his wife, Mary, both cradle Southern Baptists, decided that their new church would be primarily one that was centered on Jesus Christ, and secondly, one that required "integrity of

✦ 3. EDUCATING EVERY LAY MEMBER ✦

Newcomers to Seekers are usually sent to the church's School of Christian Living, following a long-standing Church of the Saviour tradition of educating members in the what and why of Christian living. Church members teach the classes, which are held on a semester system. "You need to know the theology before you go into community," says Marjory Bankson, who teaches in the school, which is for both members and people who are questioning. "We're not there to beat anybody up if they're not a believer." Classes are held weekly— for either six or twelve weeks—beginning with dinner at 7 P.M. and a short meditation. At Seekers, prospective members are required to take four courses from its school—Old Testament, New Testament, Christian Growth, and Christian Doctrine—which take two years to complete. Classes are also offered in everything from prayer to journal-writing to sacred dance.

The theme of close Christian community is also woven into the school, where classes are kept small to simulate a mission group experience and time is always allocated for personal sharing. "The hope is that a person gain not only intellectual understanding, but also experience confrontation with the living God," Elizabeth O'Connor, a founding member of the Church of the Saviour, wrote in *Call to Commitment,* her history of the church. "Each course is planned to lead to that most decisive of all choices: total commitment to Christ."

membership," or a real, tangible, living out of Christian beliefs in service to the poor and the marginalized.

They shopped their dream around to some of the major Christian thinkers of the time, such as Elton Trueblood and Reinhold Niebuhr, and in 1947, the Church of the Saviour was born. Gordon and Mary Cosby and Mary's sister, Elizabeth Campagna, were its only members. Gradually, others followed and a retreat center was founded on a 220-acre farm, 2025 Massachusetts Avenue was purchased, and the Potter's House opened, with a different mission group "hanging out" there each night to both discern the neighborhood's needs and to talk about the Church of the Saviour's approach to the Christian life. When riots wracked Washington in the late 1960s, the Potter's House remained open, an oasis of peace. For Love of Children (FLOC) was founded to care for unwanted or abandoned children. Church of the Saviour was by the mid-seventies a well-known stopover on many a pilgrim's journey; it had become interwoven with the fabric of Adams-Morgan. Throughout Christian America, it was held up as a model, an astounding success story.

But then, on that dramatic Sunday in 1976, Gordon Cosby acted on his instinct that the church had grown so large that the closeness that was integral to his vision was being sacrificed. He disbanded Church of the Saviour during a morning liturgy and asked the members right then to break up into smaller groups based on their interests. The members stood up, somewhat in shock, and slowly moved to different parts of the room. Six smaller churches were formed on the spot, addressing such issues as housing, jobs, health, addiction, and homelessness. One of them was Seekers, and its work, that Gordon Cosby would later call "the civil rights movement of our time," would be with children's issues.

Cosby did not know it at the time, but there would be a significant change in the people who would now come forward to be members of these Church of the Saviour offshoots. The first generation had been primarily government workers who were dissatisfied with their jobs and embraced the idea of corporate call, where an entire group worked together on one mission. The second generation had already read about that call through Elizabeth O'Connor's books on the Church of the Saviour and were ready to answer the call to their vocation—or to find work in which they could live it out.

Marjory and Peter Bankson had just moved to Washington, and like many other people, visited the Church of the Saviour after reading O'Connor's books. "I was looking for a place that valued women and didn't discount them," Marjory recalls. "This was before the women's movement was fully under way, but it was obvious that Church of the Saviour was already committed to that." There was also a paucity in leadership, as key members of the Church of the Saviour were now stretched among six churches. The Banksons jumped in, and more than twenty years later, although childless themselves, are some of the most active members of Seekers, sometimes known as the "children's church."

While the nine little churches, including Seekers, move independently, their spiritual founding father, Cosby, still preaches an ecumenical service in the long, thin parlor of 2025 Massachusetts Avenue at 11:30 on Sunday mornings. His left hand gripping the lectern and his right hand in the air to emphasize the points he has written on the pages of a yellow legal pad, his is a quiet yet commanding presence. "We are not countercultural; the gospel is countercultural and unless we stand up against the prevailing culture we are just like that salt that has lost its flavor. . . . Only when we are small, when we work in small ways, in small groups, do we really get close to people. . . . And only when we work with people who are needy, downtrodden, hungry do we get close to God. . . . And after all, which of us isn't needy, down-trodden, hungry?"

Unlike many of the well-known preachers and Christian leaders of this century who might have megachurches, a television show, and multimillion-dollar ministries, Gordon Cosby, whose methods are studied by seminaries and written about in books, is preaching to no more than a hundred people.

In midweek I join Cosby for lunch at the Potter's House, which is now looked upon as much as a pleasant, inexpensive place to eat as it is the birthplace of one of the most significant movements in Protestantism today. He is a small man with a marvelously lined face that reads like a road map of the pains inflicted by our social ills, yet has a certain blend of both optimism and humor emanating from his hooded eyes. "So, what about all this?" he says quizzically. "It amazes me, too. Vision? No, there was no great vision; in fact vision is the destroyer of essence. As visions get bigger and institutions get bigger, they lose that essence. But megachurch or tiny church; the real issue is if they take issue with the culture. Let's always be reminded that Jesus wasn't crucified because he fed the multitudes and cured the lepers. He was crucified because he was questioning the temple, the status quo, the way things were. The District of Columbia doesn't like us much because we keep on saying 'You can't treat people this way' or 'Look, people are on the street, babies are hungry.'

"But we have to be careful we just don't do the work, thinking that we are doing so much good. Without a deepening inner life it will never last. I've seen that happen so many times. We must constantly identify with the poor as Christ did but you have to realize that you too might be hung up on a cross for your efforts. But that's all right," he concludes with a sly smile, "we'll be in good company."

The demanding message of Church of the Saviour continues to be heard throughout America. Thousands of people have come through its Servant Leadership School, attended its retreats, worshiped with its tiny churches. It is not that they all go back to their lives and their churches to live exactly as women like Marjory Bankson and Sonya Dyer do. But they take back the simple lesson that to be small—and committed—can be beautiful in the eyes of God.

MountainTop Community Church

2221 Old Columbiana Road
Birmingham, AL 35216
205-823-7090
www.mountaintopchurch.com

✦ POINTS OF EXCELLENCE ✦

1. Life situation preaching

2. Modular Christian education

3. Nine hours to commitment/ministry

If architectural awards were given out for the least lovely churches in America, MountainTop Community Church would certainly be in the running. Set in a gulch at the far end of an expanse of asphalt parking lot, its members affectionately call the main building the "tire store" because of the square, high portico tacked onto the stolid, prefabricated building that houses an auditorium, gymnasium, and a few meeting rooms. Actually, the cluster of other prefabricated buildings and trailers that have crept up the hillside on either side of the main building make it look a bit more like an emergency relief compound the Red Cross might have quickly erected in some disaster area. It is all the more incongruous here in the Vestavia Hills section of Birmingham, an area rich in elegant church complexes and small, picturesque chapels.

But it was a sort of emergency that brought MountainTop into being in 1992. As Bill Elder, a Southern Baptist minister and the founding pastor puts it: "I was on my third church and, I guess, a successful career trajectory. Although people there said they wanted to do church as I had laid out my plans before they hired me, it just became harder and harder to innovate, to reach people beyond our core constituency. If I was willing to sacrifice my marriage, my children, and my stomach lining—and take ten years—I could have turned that church around. I didn't want to do any of those things, so

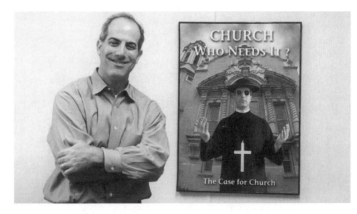

Larry Cochran, former bond-trader

I just—well—did something I never thought I would do: I went out on my own."

Bill Elder and his wife, Linda, found eight others who shared a vision of a church that would reach out to those they called "seekers," both the unchurched and those who might be called "underchurched," people tired of conventional approaches, who went to church—when they did—out of either guilt or habit, not out of passion or desire. This tiny group of ten vowed they would put aside their preconceptions of what a church, as currently constituted, could be and go back in time to Christianity's very founding. They would use the simple example of Acts 2, not denominational handbooks, creeds, or rules as both their inspiration and their guiding light. The Bible would be their only tradition.

MountainTop, in its first year, migrated among various Birmingham living rooms, then, as more people came, into the lunchroom of Berry High School, and finally the hastily constructed building that is now its home. Membership has grown to 1,500, but it is not numbers alone that set MountainTop apart. Many churches can boast of rising membership. Something transcendent has happened in the lives of hundreds of MountainTop people, something that bursts out of those prosaic aluminum walls, something they take into the world of their families, their work, their communities.

"I was your typical disaffected Protestant, going through the motions, waking up on Sunday morning and dreading going to services," says Jerry DeFoor, a forty-nine-year-old vice-president of a major Birmingham corporation. "Then I walked into MountainTop and it blew me away. Could it be this good? I couldn't wait to get back there."

As I talked with MountainTop members at their places of work and listened to the people who came to my unofficial "office" at a picnic table outside one of the newer prefabricated classroom buildings, I heard story after story, at once heartrending and heartwarming: marriages about to collapse; children with no rudder in life; unethical behavior in the workplace; addictions to drugs, alcohol, and the easy sexuality of the Internet. Stories set against backgrounds that often included some—if not intensive—religious training and practice, both Protestant and Catholic. But somehow the "faith of the fathers" had not translated or traveled well into the modern day.

"Religion in the South is too often a cultural thing, not something that is really taken into the world, or lived out in the home," says Sharon King, the thirty-nine-year-old owner of King's Kars, a used car lot set in the shadows of the expressways that slice through inner-city Birmingham. "You dress up on Sunday, smile politely, and you are strangers the rest of the week. In fact, too many churches shoulder out people who don't fit, don't dress right, or don't appear to have their lives together. I was raised a good Methodist, and when I had children, I attended, mostly for them. My daughter Raleigh was mildly mentally retarded and I always felt they barely tolerated her. Then when she was hospitalized, I didn't get a single call from this church I had been going to for years. I stopped going altogether.

"My neighbor had been bugging me about MountainTop and I finally gave in. What it was, I don't know, but I saw the face of Christ in the faces of those people, something I've never seen before in the churches I went to. They welcomed Raleigh with open arms. So it wasn't long after that I joined and became a Christian. Ah, then it began."

She smiles as she gazes out at the blighted neighborhood beyond her smudged windows, then looks down pensively upon the grease-stained carpeting. "I had this fantasy all this would change the next morning, my friends would be different, my kids would listen to me. None of that changed; but I had to. I was a foul-mouthed, sometimes mean-spirited, selfish woman who had a salesman working for me who lied and treated people like dirt, a mechanic who would do just enough to get a car running so we could sell it. That wasn't what the Bible was calling me to be."

The carpeting stubbornly maintains its grimy appearance, but Sharon King's old life has indeed changed. That salesman and mechanic are gone. She has a better relationship with both employees and customers. She still dreams of opening up a flower shop where she can be nice to everyone, but for now, she gulps and tells people honestly about the car they might buy.

The Sunday morning service that first attracted Sharon and hundreds of others is not a matter of chance, but of a strategy of Bill Elder's to make seekers feel "totally comfortable, anonymous, nonthreatened financially or liturgically." It is a service, the church has vowed, "in which they will be impressed by the relevancy of message, moved by the music, stimulated by the question raised in the drama, impressed with the commitment to excellence, and one from which they can go away with some very helpful insight on living. We want them to come back on their own." And, a church vision statement adds, "No pews, no pipe organ, no jacket required."

For sure, a MountainTop Sunday morning worship is certainly not what most congregants grew up with. Coming into the "tire store," worshipers are warmly greeted and ushered into an auditorium that does not have a single religious symbol: no cross, no altar, no pulpit. In fact, no minister. On the Sunday I visit, the service begins with a skit about three types of preachers—Sominex (putting people to sleep), Terminex (fire and brimstone), and Feel Good. Larry Cochran (in real life, a bond-trader who took a two-thirds pay cut to work in the church's financial administration) plays the preachers in comic overstatement: the first boring, the second berating, and the third drifting across the stage trailing bubbles in his wake. Jon Nickerson, as a sort of Everyman stage manager, quietly talks about another preacher two thousand years ago who "made being good attractive. He was recruiting pioneers to talk about a new kind of world." The day's scripture, the story of Peter letting down the nets on Jesus' bidding—after Peter had unsuccessfully fished those very waters—is read.

The curtain opens on an eight-person rock band of teenagers and twenty-somethings, but including a quite mature male dentist and a female physician who is the mother of two. Lead singer Jon Nickerson—a heartthrob himself—belts out "Saddle up your horses. We've got a trail to blaze." The audio is flawless, the banks of stage lights perfectly balanced. Then, a few congregational songs, upbeat tunes easily learned, with words projected on a screen overhead. There are neither hymnals nor books of prayer available.

A full half hour into the service, Bill Elder, in slacks and a button-down shirt open at the neck, nonchalantly walks onto the stage, almost as if he has just happened upon the place. The title of the sermon is "Pioneering," but Elder begins several rungs down the emotional ladder by suggesting the emptiness that many of them might be feeling. "We want more, we want new experiences, but we're armchair pioneers." It just won't work that way is the apparent conclusion.

He is a handsome man, tall, thin, with neatly parted gray hair. His easy style, with no visible speaking notes, belies a man who in an average week spends some twenty hours in sermon preparation. The front end of the sermon could easily be construed as a lesson in secular self-help, but once the connective tissue is made between the tepid faith of the men

Modular, modern Christian education

in that boat and the scriptural admonition to cast a new net, the remainder of the sermon is solidly, biblically based.

"God is in the business of filling empty vessels," he says. Throughout the church heads are down, as notes—an amazing occurrence in any preacher's life—are being taken. "If Jesus fills you with that faith, you've got to give up comfort and control. But with this faith, this trust, you become a pioneer, a faith pioneer."

"Did Bill Elder call my wife?" or "Was Bill Elder peeking through my windows this week?" are typical responses I heard from congregants who, week after week, find their pastor's preaching like a laser beam piercing their souls, their family crises, their needs at work, their spiritual hunger.

"Yes, I know we are doing things very differently, but the first thing you have to do is get people's attention," Bill Elder says over brunch at the nearby Hotel Winfrey, as the

✦ 1. Life Situation Preaching ✦

"We're not talking hermeneutics or creationism or how this translates from the Aramaic," says Bill Elder. "At Mountain-Top our sermons, our talks before small groups are about life application; that's what people are hungering for today. How do I live my life, how do I make my family work in a profoundly secular culture? We are in a prosperous city, Birmingham, but make no mistake, this is a missionary church. There is impoverishment in many forms. We always say we are building our church for people we don't know yet. There are one hundred thousand of them not more than ten miles from our door. People are hurt, unaware of their predicament, unaware that it is only God who will fill that black hole that exists within each of us. They want to do better with their kids, they want to get off the treadmill and make their work life more meaningful. Peace, love, wholeness —you can't get these just by being successful in the world. All a pastor has to do is be aware of what his people are going through and address those issues—that is life situation preaching."

conversation ranges from where he has come from, denominationally, to where he hopes to travel, spiritually. "I'm sad to report that we have a dysfunctional family within the Southern Baptist church today, fighting battles that are not important and neglecting to provide what people need to survive. Here at MountainTop, we're not reinventing the church from scratch. We're going back to scratch, to the basics. Small groups, accountability, sharing our resources, prayer, rule by consensus and by elders who rise up from the congregation. We may look very hip and millennial, but we really are pretty old-fashioned.

"There are so many seekers and so few seeker-sensitive churches like ours and do you know why? Because this takes a lot more work. Everything we do, we do with great care, thought, planning. We don't do prepackaged Sunday school for adults, we do Applied Biblical Christianity seminars. Our kids come on Sunday morning or Sunday evening and they get a first-class presentation of Bible values. They might have three or four activities in their hour: art, a drama, a multimedia production. We are not competing against other churches, we are competing against Hollywood for their attention.

"So, we hire good staff and we pay them. We don't just hope that a volunteer will fill a slot and toss a course book at them. This kind of church allows for no coasting by me and the staff." And this is decidedly not "Christianity Lite," he says, countering the criticisms of his and other churches of the Willow Creek–model that have sprung up in the past thirty years and gained hundreds of thousands of followers.

Willow Creek Community Church (www.willowcreek.org is a wealth of information) began in 1975 and has grown into an international movement of seeker-sensitive churches. Located in South Barrington, Illinois, it draws thousands to weekly services and provides resources for churches in the United States and abroad. Oddly enough, when Bill Elder first met with that group of ten to discuss a new kind of church, he had never heard of Willow Creek, yet found he was following a similar path to a church that was at once culturally relevant yet doctrinally pure.

"We are a church that believes that by impacting the family, we impact society," says Elder. "It is my hope—and I do hear this—that MountainTop persons stand out, stand for

✦ 2. MODULAR CHRISTIAN EDUCATION ✦

"We are a seeker-targeted church and many of the kids who come on Sundays are not used to the typical Sunday school, so we don't jump right into something religious," says Amy Freels, MountainTop's director of children's ministries. Amy and her staff will have three different small-group activities—for example, the children will dig through sand like archaeologists to find buried artifacts, so they get a feel of what might go on in the Holy Land, move on to paint a Wall of Jericho, and then construct a map of Israel with water, desert, and mountains. After a dramatization of the Bible lesson, the children then move into small groups to discuss what they did, what they saw, and to ask questions. This modular approach is sensitive to a young child's short attention span, while presenting a rich, hands-on approach to learning biblical lessons and stories.

something, are not only proud of their church, but that leaven in their home, their place of work, wherever they are. We do our services well, we do education well, but the real key to this is our small groups. It's a kind of intimacy you'll never get in a Sunday school class. It's true accountability—to the Bible, to each other. This is where God really works on people."

Besides Sharon King, two type A males, Sam Corona and Bruce Brandenburg, are good examples of the transforming power of this church and those small groups. Sam, a Birmingham-born and -bred Catholic (who sadly admits he met more people in the first ten minutes on his first Sunday at MountainTop than he did in the previous ten years attending Catholic churches), tells me, "I was making money hand over fist, out with my buddies, playing golf, drinking, swearing, and I kept wondering why I wasn't happy? I've got it all! I owned a business and I was treating people badly, I never had any time for my family, and I was completely sucked into the material world. I wanted all the toys.

"It was actually my son who first came to MountainTop with a friend and I had never seen him that enthusiastic about religion before. Then I came to MountainTop and got into a Bible study group. Catholics don't know the Bible and I had never known about this kind of fellowship, about guys I could really talk to about what was going on in my life, not just the Auburn football game." Now, this Catholic, Sam Corona, who was never so much as on a committee, is leading a David group for sexual purity and participating in three Bible study groups. "The Bible refreshes me, focuses me. I see my old drinking buddies and I just want to tell them what they're missing. There's something about keeping that 'edge,' going outside your comfort zone to try to be fair, listen to your kids, watch your language. It's not fun as I knew fun before, but this really feels good. This is not about rules, it's about where your heart is."

Bruce Brandenburg was an equally hard-driving young executive, a man with a reputation for enjoying the cut-throat, high-stakes environment of commercial banking. He had a huge house, no friends, and a terrible reputation among the employees he supervised. His marriage was in jeopardy. His children were strangers. After joining a small group and finding a supportive environment, he began to open up, first about his deteriorating relationship with his oldest daughter. Bruce, who easily could make employees cry, now shed his own tears. He shared his struggles, as did other members of the group, and a new man began to form.

When he got into his car to drive to a leadership conference at Willow Creek a year later he was a new man, beloved by fellow workers who had been touched by his new concern for them, not only for their job performance. His marriage was repaired and he was closer to his children. Crossing the state of Indiana, Bruce apparently fell asleep at the wheel of his car and was killed. His wife, Bobbi, was already at the conference, where she received the tragic news.

"Horrible, it was just horrible," Bobbi Brandenburg recalls to the members of her small group as we sit together on a Sunday evening. "But I couldn't think of where I would rather be. I was surrounded by my community, people who cared about me, who helped shape both me and Bruce. Bruce was a man who learned to practice God's presence and you people around me continually do the same thing."

MountainTop people feel they have found not only a church home, but a real community. Many of them are miles away from their extended families. The neighborhoods of leisurely evening walks and front-porch sentinels have been replaced by a mobile lifestyle, the pressures of a two-income life, microwave meals on the run, too much time in the SUV taking kids to soccer, dance, and Scouts.

"This is a church that is willing to go through the terrible times in your life and not abandon you," one man tells me. He had been fired from his job because he inflated sales figures to meet a mandated target. Embarrassed and humiliated, he called his wife, ready to just drive off, leaving everything. Minutes later, his cell phone rang and he looked down to see "MountainTop" on the screen. "It was instinctual," his wife tells me. "Instead of calling nine-one-one, I dialed eight-two-three-seven-zero-nine-zero." She had called the church's number, and minutes later Bill Elder was on the phone to her husband, telling him he wasn't alone in his darkest hour. And when Elder and the man's small-group leader met at his home an hour later it was, as the man tells me, "to listen and to love me, not to judge. 'God will restore you,' they said, and that's what happened."

One's man's daughter was anorexic; another man was addicted to Internet sex; an unmarried couple was living together; another couple started their marriage in a bar, but knew it couldn't flourish in such places. "This was my family —perhaps even at times more accepting than my family," says a grateful man who shall remain nameless.

While MountainTop is a seekers' oasis where the community generously offers comfort, it is also a church of demands. MountainTop is not about well-intentioned but often empty religious platitudes but tireless self-examination, accountability, "keeping the edge," as more than one member tells me.

That "edge," or "practicing God's presence," is reinforced in Sunday services, dealt with in more personal ways during small-group discussions, and continually tested in the world. When a MountainTop member who is a physical therapist supervisor told a prospective job applicant the advertised job opening was filled, he knew he did so because the voice was that of an African American. He knew this racist act didn't square with what he'd talked about in his small group the week before—and he surely didn't want to have to confess it the next week. He called right back and asked the person in for an interview. When a nurse's supervisor falsely accused her of grabbing the spotlight at a meeting, this feisty woman, who once lived on a kibbutz in Israel said nothing and let it pass, offering it up. These acts are small, but they are the acts of heroism, the little murders or moments of grace that are the warp and woof of our lives.

From its very inception—in fact the very reason for its founding—Bill Elder and those first MountainTop founders dreamed of becoming fundamentalists in the most fundamental of ways: to live in the current day as the disciples did two thousand years ago, to be an Acts 2 congregation. When issues come up, these modern men and women hearken back to ancient ways—they don't hold more meetings or commission studies and surveys; they pray together. They avoid the myriad of boards and commissions that strangle many a church, allowing elders (there are now three) to make decisions about issues that cannot be settled by consensus of the individuals involved. As for intercession, MountainTop members go directly to those who are having marital or financial or emotional difficulties. They are decidedly *not* strangers to each other throughout the week.

If the simplicity and directness of MountainTop's governance and intercessions are admirable, the complexity of its many education and outreach classes is equally impressive. Questioners who are not sure if they want to be a part of this church, in fact wondering if there is a God at all, can attend Rob Lagerstrom's "Facts on Faith" discussion group. After expressing interest in joining MountainTop, new members are whisked into nine hours of tutelage on membership, spiritual maturity, and the discernment of the right ministry for them. Sunday morning services are for seekers and members, Wednesday night is tailored more for members and even broken down again into three individual services for different age groups.

I sit in wonder during a middle school–age class as Zacheus, Eve, Jonah, and Elisha tell of the God they know. These videotaped "interviews" had been prepared during the week and would be used for this Sunday alone. The next

Sunday the innovative staff led by Amy Freels would think of still other ways to present the gospel message.

That evening, during a youth group gathering dealing with the vicissitudes of temporal acclaim and acceptance, each teenager is given a paper crown, symbolizing what the world might promise. They are invited to approach a fire blazing in an outdoor grill and allow those crowns to go up in smoke. Then, they are given a symbolic gold ring and a scriptural passage, 1 Corinthians 3:10–13, providing a tactful, tactile way to express that God has even greater riches in store for them.

As Bridget Butts, a vivacious seventeen-year-old high school senior tells me, "MountainTop is the cool place to be for kids. Kids will come to church if parents force them, but nobody has to be forced to come here. This is good for us and we realize it; we're learning how to make our lives better. I used to go to all the parties; there was plenty of drinking and drugs were around. I don't go anymore and it's easier to have a reason not to go. That's just not where God wants me to be."

At the end of my stay I arrive at the New York Bagel Cafe & Deli on Acton Road for the 6:30 Monday morning Bible study group of which Sam Corona is a member. I am a little early, and when I see three men at a table with Bibles open, I ask "MountainTop?" No, they answer. There are two other tables with two men apiece at them, but they are not the MountainTop group either. Finally Sam arrives. So, in New York Bagel Cafe & Deli at 6:30 on a Monday morning there are no fewer than four men's Bible study groups. It sinks in; this *is* the Bible Belt. The Bible is common currency here. Whether or not it permeates lives is, of course, an entirely different issue.

✦ 3. NINE HOURS TO COMMITMENT/ MINISTRY ✦

MountainTop's core curriculum of Christian discipleship, called Life Discovery and Development, is a well-planned, concise program that takes the churched or unchurched through three steps, from initial interest in the church to complete involvement in MountainTop ministries. The first two-hour seminar "Discovering MCC Membership" is designed to teach people considering membership what the church is about and what is expected of members. "Discovering Spiritual Maturity," the second seminar, is three hours long and introduces the six habits of a spiritually alive and growing Christian, showing that commitment is a process, not an end point. Then, in "Discovering My Ministry," a two-evening, four-hour seminar, people discover their own distinctive spiritual profile and through it find their ministry niche at MountainTop.

But as these eight men from MountainTop bite into both their bagels and the Acts 8 stories of the spread of Christianity in Samarian villages, they ponder how they will take their beliefs into a morning meeting of an advertising staff, the stops a rug salesman will make, Sam's business calls to sell his new line of ergonomic chairs, and a high-tech research lab. They are imperfect men, they are the first to admit. But there is something enormously appealing about both their honesty and their desire to live better lives. These are not pious or "churchy" men, but men you would be glad to know, have working beside you, or living next door.

Although their church is growing and it is successful, many MountainTop members know it is imperfect too. The lack of religious symbols bother some of them, as do the infrequency of the Lord's Supper and the fact that their predominantly white youth group hasn't yet been taken to Birmingham's excellent Civil Rights Museum to be confronted with the tawdry racial legacy of this city, once known as "Bombingham." Even the fact that a new multimillion-dollar church complex is now under construction gives them a moment to pause. Will they succumb to the very institutionalism that many of them had escaped? Will they persist in staying in their own economic and racial comfort zone? Will they lose the edge altogether?

Yet, there is something infectious here, something you cannot help wanting to be a part of. MountainTop is both impressive and an infant church, a work in progress. It is a success and it is a church of broken people, continually open about their brokenness.

And about a cross for this wonderful church, to make a statement to the world? Perhaps it is not so much an issue of putting off that decision for a church that has reached so deeply into so many lives and the very fabric of this city. Perhaps it is a symbol yet to be earned.

4

All Saints Episcopal Church

10 Irving Place
Worcester, MA 01609
508-752-3766
www.allsaintschurchworc.org

✦   POINTS OF EXCELLENCE   ✦

1. Different approaches to spirituality

2. Linking church power to city needs

3. Need for and use of clerical sabbatical

Near the corner of Pleasant Street, the imposing Chestnut Street Congregational Church presides majestically over downtown Worcester, Massachusetts. With its huge spire, commanding turrets, paneled walls, and ample pews, this architectural

A choir more than one hundred years old

gem was always considered *the* mother church of Worcester Protestants, home to its wealthiest and most influential citizens. What could prevail against such a paean to God's power and man's homage?

While the church's outward appearance is still impressive, within, the pews are dusty, offices abandoned, classrooms empty—as they have been for more than fifteen years.

A tall, bearded man whose clerical collar is partially hidden beneath his windbreaker stares up pensively at this grand edifice on a blustery fall afternoon. He is walking these streets with members of his congregation as they assess what they have done and what they have failed to do in this, their ecclesial neighborhood. And Rev. Mark Beckwith cannot pass Chestnut Street Congregational without pausing for an examination of conscience—and purpose. As pastor of All Saints Episcopal, another of the grand churches built about the city's center more than a century before, he is most aware that downtown churches are an endangered species within mainline Protestantism.

Mark Beckwith knew all too well that three of these grand, downtown Worcester churches had already closed when he came here six years before. He was determined that his new assignment, All Saints, just a block and a half away, would not meet a similar, ignominious fate. This was not to be just a holding action, he and his associate pastor, Rev. Becky Brown, vowed. They were not there to carefully "package" Jesus for a comfortable congregation of ever-declining numbers and ever-increasing average age. The music and liturgy of All Saints had always been exceptional, but Mark and Becky dreamed of moving beyond the walls of All Saints, undertaking nothing short of the revitalization of the city blocks that radiate out from All Saints. The bodegas of Pleasant Street, the housing projects, the retirement high-rise: these too were their parish.

As for this complete revitalization of downtown Worcester, as of this writing, Mark and Becky have—of course—failed.

But All Saints has proved to be a beacon of hope for downtown Worcester's core, a welcoming presence for the landed gentry and landless immigrants, a powerful, unapologetically religious presence that has made a bold statement to stay rooted in this ever-changing neighborhood.

Its legendary boys choir, established more than a hundred years ago, still enchants worshipers; its liturgical pomp and circumstance are a tribute to the best in Episcopal practice. But its members standing before a public housing block to reconsecrate the ground after a drive-by shooting send still another message. A 9:30 Sunday morning "family-friendly" service, which some members describe—and not always apologetically—as "barely Episcopal," draws new and enthusiastic young families. The after-church welcoming for new members, once called "Huntington Hell"—after the lifeless formality that was begrudgingly staged in Huntington Hall—has turned into a fun-filled hour. A medieval labyrinth painted by the youth group provides a slant on spirituality few members have experienced.

"The issue is whether our church serves as temple or synagogue," Mark Beckwith says as we sit in his sun-drenched office
one morning during my visit. "The temple is beautiful, a
museum, where ritual is everything. Or the synagogue where
teaching and learning goes on, where the living of the word is
not only preached, but where we take what we have to the
streets, not just lock it up inside and tell each other how right
and wonderful we are and how awful the world is outside. In
today's Protestant world, temples die and synagogues live."

All Saints is, without reservation, a breathtakingly beautiful church. Its high-vaulted, wood-paneled ceiling soars over
hand-carved pews and choir stalls. The sixty-ton marble rere-
dos elegantly depicting the epiphany, crucifixion, and resur-
rection stand behind the altar demanding both awe and
reverence. After all, this was once a church where ushers
served in morning coats, the vestry met in the Worcester
Club, and talking about the problems of the surrounding
neighborhood was considered exceedingly bad form.

The painful transition from old church to new church has
proved to be one that many a mainstream Protestant congregation—and individual members—are unable or unwilling
to make. And perhaps George Bernardin can be considered
representative of the Episcopal "hinge" generation, those
raised in this wonderful tradition, but who have made a successful passage to a new and vibrant expression of their faith.

"Let's be honest," George confides, "for older Episcopalians, church was not about a great emotional, or even religious, connection. It was more cultural, social. But that day is
over." George is a handsome, gray-haired, retired industrial
executive. "To say that we older Episcopalians are now somehow so spiritually enlightened wouldn't exactly be correct. I
still daydream during sermons; I'm not really cerebral. But I
think people like myself have discovered that we are part of

God's imagination, and the Spirit of God is everywhere, not in rules and regulations. We could live without a church, sure, but we have found that the institutional church is good, necessary for society. The church—this church—goes places that get short shrift elsewhere. And it is our job as people of faith to teach people how to behave in a civilized society, the difference between right and wrong—not by preaching to them on Sunday morning, but living it out every day of the week.

"We are the only downtown church with a significant number of black members—in fact, church membership goes back six generations in our oldest family, which is black—and we have the means to make things happen. We can't just talk to each other anymore; we have to empower other groups to have their own voices. Government responds to squeaky wheels, so we have to be those squeaky wheels. And believe me, that is neither easy nor is it painless. Going out into those streets wasn't the most natural thing for us, but it became apparent that's exactly what God was calling us to do."

The dramatic march and liturgy that members of All Saints held after the drive-by shooting of eighteen-year-old Nik Diaz was a product of the kind of outreach this church has pioneered under Mark Beckwith. Yolanda Matias, forty-two, was a member of the congregation but also a cleaning lady for some of its members and a sextant at the church. When she and her daughter were pinned down by gunshots one night on Newberry Street, the church decided to listen to one of its own and take action.

"It was straightforward enough," says Mark Beckwith. "This was happening to one of our members and her neighbors. We first talked to some of the residents and then went to that block to pray with them. We held prayer vigils for four weeks to stand with them against the violence that was so pervasive in their lives. When Nik Diaz was shot, although we didn't know him personally, the neighborhood did, and we had to do something. We already had some credibility because of the prayer vigils so we did what we do best. We created a liturgy to honor him and to express our solidarity with the people. Yes, I know something like this could be considered risky, but we have to try different approaches, different ways to get to the center we are all seeking."

The once-blood-drenched sidewalk on Chatham Street became its own sanctuary, the setting for a touching liturgy. Many an Episcopalian who had once only driven through this neighborhood with doors locked and eyes fixed ahead now stood together with people they knew not by name, but by compassion and need. Holy water reconsecrated the spot where Nik died. More than one hundred neighborhood people stood shoulder to shoulder with the people of All Saints. And with the parting words of the hymn "City of God," they sang together, "May our tears be turned into dancing."

"At first I thought this All Saints was a little too high class and snooty, but they proved who they were when they came out to the streets," says Yolanda. "I really felt the church was there for me when it really counted. This was my support, my strength, my family."

Doris Buell is another long-standing All Saints member, and she is more than willing to point out that government programs will never take the place of what a church can do. "Secular good will is wonderful, but it is like a cut flower, which will look good and last only for a while, because it has no roots. Our church is a living plant, with deep roots in this community. We have been here, are here now, and will be here—God willing—for years to come."

Meredyth Ward discovered the welcome of All Saints in two dramatically different ways: the acceptance of women as lay leaders and the acceptance of her interracial family. "I

✦ 1. DIFFERENT APPROACHES TO SPIRITUALITY ✦

At All Saints, pastor Mark Beckwith is a believer that "although we often don't know exactly where we're going or if we are doing exactly the right thing, we have to try different approaches, different ways if we are to demonstrate to the world—and to ourselves—that churches can transform lives and society." From the service at the site of a murder to the youth group's painting of a labyrinth to use as a spiritual path for congregants to drastically different Sunday morning services for children, as well as one for more traditional members, All Saints is not afraid to redraw its institutional and spiritual template. "We will make mistakes, that's a given, but without trying new ways to reach people, we have never really put faith to the test."

received the best in Roman Catholic training at Holy Cross College, then at a Jesuit theological school," Meredyth, forty-four, says, "only to find that there were no jobs for people like me in the Catholic church. I went to other churches with my children and felt less than welcome. We were different; we didn't fit the comfortable pattern. I came to All Saints and they were eager to have me teach, participate. And I looked around on Sunday morning and my multihued family was nothing out of the ordinary. I had found a new home. There is just a different way of being a church here.

"And what was immediately impressive was that this was a church willing to stick its neck out, take chances. The church helped to bring over a family from Kosovo, but when they finally found an affordable place to live and were presented with a lease, there was no way a landlord was going to approve them. The church cosigned that lease. This wasn't just some liberal, flighty decision; we really worked it through so that we were both charitable and responsible. We faced that tension and got it done. To me we were a 'sacred bridge,' which is exactly what we need between the church and the world."

"I've spent my life involved in good causes and that was important to me about All Saints," says Paul Reville, a Harvard educational reform specialist. "But what really attracted me was that Mark and Becky were really connected to God. God was the crucial part of the equation. God was at the center of their sermons. For twenty minutes each Sunday, I heard not only about what we needed to do, but the God that was with us. We sometimes tend to forget about the most important element of all."

For Brian Litzenberger, who came to the church because he was attracted by its music program, All Saints has proved not to be a safe haven in the midst of a turbulent world, "but a place where members can fight with each other, disagree—and sometimes bitterly disagree on what and if we should be doing certain things—and yet stay connected. If Mark has taught us anything, it is to stay connected and we can work anything out."

Raised in upper-middle-class privilege in Darien, Connecticut, Mark Beckwith was raised in the kind of cultural Episcopalianism George Bernardin talks about. Then came the Vietnam War, and Mark, then a freshman at Amherst College, saw that the hermetically sealed life he had lived was far removed from the larger American experience and that the values so many people talked about were little more than cocktail-party patter. After two years in Japan, he entered Yale Divinity School and eventually served two churches as an associate. He began to see clearly how he wanted to express his ministry. His first rectorship was in Hackensack, New Jersey, in a church virtually given up for dead. Not only did he revitalize the church, but he also helped start the Interreligious Fellowship for the Homeless in Bergen County, which eventually grew to involve some two hundred congregations and five thousand volunteers in providing shelter, food, and affordable housing for the homeless.

When All Saints opened up, Mark was one of three finalists. As search committee members recall, he did not pull any punches; he was the candidate who promised to push them the hardest.

Once in Worcester, he looked both inwardly to All Saints' church life and outwardly to the crumbling neighborhood that surrounded it and decided he had to work on both fronts at once. "You need a strong church commitment to support social action or else you just run out of steam—and grace. We

learned that lesson all too well in the seventies. Healthy church life is crucial and you have to keep on trying to feed people so that they have the strength to live out the gospel. But you can't just do it the same old ways. For some, the *Book of Common Prayer* is exactly right; for others, we have to"—he smiles—"adapt a bit."

As people gather for the 9:30 A.M. liturgy one Sunday, I notice it is certainly a rich

Len Berry at the shelter

amalgam of humanity. Blue-blooded members in penny loafers mix with a street person with clothes of a style and color that went out of fashion a few seasons ago. White children, black children, and mixed-race children mingle naturally as happy congregants. The "sermon" is rendered by Strong Eagle Daly, a Native American with a bristly, narrow hedge of hair atop an otherwise shaved head. There are some words about love and harmony, perhaps a bit more about Buddhism and Native American spirituality than Christianity, but the haunting notes from his double-barreled flute speak of universal truths.

At the end of the service, all children are given cymbals and rhythm sticks to make their joyful—if dissonant—noise to the hymn "Soon and Very Soon." Not typical Episcopal fare, but then again All Saints doesn't pride itself on being typical anything.

In the downstairs hall, a freshly painted labyrinth snakes its way about three huge pieces of canvas. The youth group had found the pattern, learned about the spiritual history and impact of the labyrinth, drawn the outline from an ancient formula, and then carefully painted it.

Becky Brown has conducted a very proper 7:45 Eucharist, and the 10:30 Eucharist has a similarly traditional feel. But Mark Beckwith's sermon for the feast of Christ the King minces no words. Quoting from that soaring testament to greed, *Bonfire of the Vanities,* he says that the main character Sherman McCoy's admonition to "insulate, insulate, insulate" is not what the gospel demands. Their king does not isolate himself on a throne but stoops to be with his people. Theirs is a God who asks them to open their eyes to the world around them. The royalty of this building and the economically compromised neighborhood are to be joined.

Not only has All Saints reconformed its liturgical life and

reached out to draw in young and mixed families, Mark Beckwith has also consciously targeted people whom he sensed had religious backgrounds and were doing the kind of work he wanted to accomplish in the neighborhood. One of them is Peter Fellenz, who was with Mark when he paused before Chestnut Street Congregational on that pensive walk. Fellenz, who heads a nonprofit corporation and is one of the most active players in the rehabilitation of dilapidated or abandoned homes in the city center, is now an All Saints member.

Also along was Patricia Cushman-Ton, who took on a somewhat inglorious task, then cut and plowed her way through city bureaucracy to plant dozens of easily-emptied, attractive containers so that trash might be part of a collection, not dispersed to blow about the city streets. Judy Brown-Cahill helps provide shelter for recovering homeless women, Sharon Smith-Viles works with Abbey's House for abused women, and Len Berry, who says he's in the furniture business, spends considerable time at a homeless shelter for men.

It is this kind of lay synergy that Mark Beckwith has fostered, the kind of partnership that All Saints has forged with city agencies and foundations to work in this neighborhood.

"Downtown churches are so crucially important, not just to denominational prestige, but because they are the very soul of our cities," says Mark. "We can build new structures and our wonderful new medical center in downtown Worcester, but without vibrant churches, the very lifeblood is lacking. Today cities are the new wilderness, the wasteland. But it is a wasteland with abundance, possibilities. It is here that we have to overcome and sanctify the elements. Churches can make the kind of investment in communities that no municipal, state, or federal government is ever going to make. We have great people, but we also have our tradition —too often overlooked in a day when we want immediate

✦ 2. LINKING CHURCH POWER TO CITY NEEDS ✦

"The health of this church is interwoven with the health of the neighborhood that surrounds us," says Pastor Mark Beckwith. "We feed each other or we denigrate each other. Walk out any door in this church and you see boarded-up buildings, trash, lives on the margin. What we have inside the church we must take out and what is outside we must bring in. This is not noblesse oblige; this is our biblical mandate." When Mark and other Christian and Jewish clergy discovered that 80 percent of local schoolchildren turn over each year, they went to the city to see what they could do to help stabilize this chaotic situation. Downtown housing, park benches, a basketball court—whatever the found need, All Saints went to work on it.

results, when we worship start-up ways as if the new was the divine. We have Sacramentals, we have the Gospels, and both are sources of endless insight. Tradition is here to be used.

"But these big churches take patience and time. I compare my church in Hackensack to an attack boat: it was easy to navigate, make quick moves, changes. A venerable institution like All Saints is more like a supertanker, able to deliver a lot more goods, but it takes a lot more time to get it to turn." As we sit talking, this time in the back of his vacant, cavernous, and gorgeous church late on a Monday afternoon, Mark Beckwith looks about pensively.

"It's not just about a congregation being adverse to change; we in the ministry are no different. We like our comfortable patterns; our ways of coping—or not coping—with stress, challenges, life itself. We are just as reluctant as the congregation to step outside our personal comfort zone. That's why I so needed to get away, which I did last year, for a four-month sabbatical. I didn't go to workshops or for advanced studies; in fact I doubt if I learned anything at all about the techniques of being a pastor. What this type A personality learned at Iona and Taizé was the value of silence, the value of *not* doing something, of waiting before the Lord. Then I could come back, refreshed, open to what we need to do."

Meredyth Ward looks at her new church home and compares it to "how children play house; we play kingdom. The problem with mainline churches is that they are not clear about what they are. They are no longer social clubs." Sam Pickens, a seventy-two-year-old physician, adds, "We are trying to be a symbol of a different way of doing things, that city on a hill, light in the darkness. We gather wildly different people together into a community and believe me, this is not always peaceful coexistence."

"But that's the beauty of a downtown church," adds Mark Beckwith. "It has almost chromosomal ability to absorb many different types."

Late one evening at All Saints, members of the Hands, Feet, and Heart of Christ group gather for the sixth in a series of discernment sessions to see what they should be doing in their neighborhood. Some of them have driven in from suburban homes; others moved back into the city to be close to the church. With a thick demographic study and a huge map of their neighborhood, they are united in their desire to make a difference. Characteristically for the new All Saints, their church is not at the map's center, but just one piece of a mosaic of churches and community organizations that make up this part of the city.

✦ 3. Need for and use of clerical sabbatical ✦

"Too many church people—myself sometimes included—are 'functional atheists,' to borrow Parker Palmer's term," says Mark Beckwith. "We say we believe in God, but we act as though he doesn't exist. We think we're the CEO of our local church, when in fact he is. That's why it's so important for clergy to take sabbaticals, have a jubilee, a chance to gain some perspective on what we are about. This time shouldn't be about doing anything productive, not about reading the umpteen books you have beside your bed. My time at Taizé and Iona and other holy places allowed me to get away from the Babel of needs that a downtown church is and to connect with God at the deepest level. Then, when you come back you might have something to say to your congregation about what that means."

Horns blare as night descends on Worcester. Before anything else, a scripture passage is read and quietly contemplated: the parable of Jesus asleep in the boat as a storm came up. City sounds of a warm fall night mingle with hopes and dreams of a dozen people. Worcester may not know or even care that All Saints is talking about its rebirth—the inner-city poor have heard of too many programs, too many plans to pay much attention to such pipe dreams—but there they are, their light streaming out of the windows onto Pleasant Street.

5

Riverside Baptist Church

2401 Alcott

Denver, CO 80211

303-433-8665

www.riversidebaptist.com

✦ POINTS OF EXCELLENCE ✦

1. Providing necessary support for new satellite churches

2. Worship is their "front door"

3. Effective media; 80 percent come this way

I t is a group of disciples gathered around a table perhaps as unlikely as those at the Last Supper. Some wear well-pressed, expensive suits and starched shirts and others well-wrinkled wash-and-wear trousers and T-shirts. Some hair is so neatly trimmed it could pass military muster. A ponytail dangles over the back of one flannel shirt, set off by two rivers of brightly embroidered suspenders that sweep over an ample girth, tugging only partially successfully at a pair of faded jeans far below.

It is the monthly gathering of the "ministers"—and that term must be used in quotes—of Riverside Baptist Church. If Denver's 2.4 million people represent a polyglot of races and cultures, the churched, unchurched, and prechurched, the men gathered around this table are just as diverse. They are a sign—if not to the nation (yet), then certainly to this, the Mile High City, that Riverside Baptist, once an establishment bastion, once on the verge of closing for intimating that it was the white middle class who would populate the kingdom—that big, mainline churches set in now-working-class neighborhoods can flourish. Hard by the Twenty-third Street off-ramp, its huge red-neon sign unapologetically blazing out over I-25, Riverside is testimony to a new spirit, based on ancient values. For Riverside has evolved from a moribund and stylized church to one at once vital and varied in its approaches. Riverside would not claim to be seeker-sensitive and does not shy away from its Southern Baptist Convention affiliation and Southern Baptist values—Bible inerrancy, salvation through Jesus Christ alone. But it is, in essence, a postdenominational church building upon its strong fundamentalist, evangelical foundation to reach out to new constituencies, plant new churches, and successfully implement what might best be called "niche evangelism."

I sit with the Riverside pastor, Rick Ferguson—whose type-A-personality-induced bleeding ulcer some ten years ago convinced him that he was not going about his ministry in the most effective way—in an office overlooking a Denver now bathed in dusk's fading light. As he tells of his experiences, Riverside is not portrayed as some sort of wonder

Choir practice: a mini-church service

church with only success stories and no failures. "We are making an impact, yes, I think we are," he begins slowly. He is a deliberate man, both in his speech and attire: a shirt so crisp it looks as though he just put it on and a haircut that appears no more than minutes old. "But we've had our crash and burns also. We have twenty-four different churches that appeal to different ethnic and cultural types, but we also are trying to be unified with each other. That's missionary country out there," he says, his eyes searching the blinking city lights, the tall buildings, the suburban areas where light and the gospel have not yet penetrated. "Denver is a boomtown, but ninety percent of those people are unchurched, researchers tell us. We just have to find ways to reach them. At one time my greatest dream was to have our gorgeous, bowl-shaped sanctuary, with its three thousand nicely padded seats, filled to capacity for two services every Sunday. But it dawned on me that that wasn't the answer anymore. Even two jammed services— that's six thousand people and that's Sunday morning only. We had to go out beyond this sanctuary and contextualize the ministry without compromising the message. We had to go to the people rather than expect them to come to us. 'Go' not 'come' is the great command of Jesus."

The classic model for starting new mainline denominational churches has usually been more about demographics —as visualized by a national planning office—than about discernment of the spirit—as felt by real people in a specific place. Riverside uses a more immediate and local approach, finding "islands of hope," some of which might not fit in with the primarily middle- to upper-class crowd that had once filled its Sunday services. Denver, with its abundance of good jobs, majestic scenery, and proximity to the ski slopes, has attracted people of all ages and ethnic groups, who— Ferguson began to realize—speak too many languages and come from too many cultures for one church to reach all of them in one Sunday service.

Riverside first got its taste of that when a group of non-English-speaking Koreans began attending church. "They would sit through the service, week after week, but obviously didn't understand it and couldn't really participate," Ferguson says. "Yet they were there, they kept coming." So the church bought headsets for the families, and each week, as Rick preached, a bilingual church member simultaneously translated the sermon. While that bridged a language barrier, there was much more to actually being a church, so the Koreans eventually started their own congregation, affiliated with Riverside.

Now, the church's congregations include Indonesian, Vietnamese, and Cambodian fellowships. Riverside, a fifty-year-old church with established staff and resources, furnishes the money, resources, and facilities, if necessary, for new congregations. The Riverside staff uses the analogy of a wheel, where Riverside is the hub and the satellite churches are the spokes. "We help new congregations by providing

✦ 1. PROVIDING NECESSARY SUPPORT FOR NEW SATELLITE CHURCHES ✦

After watching several would-be pastors fail at starting churches, the staff at Riverside realized that though these men were certainly well-intentioned, they might not have had the charisma and leadership skills to organize and mobilize a group of people well enough to form a church. Others didn't understand the hurdles and isolation that comes with pastorhood, the family and financial sacrifices that have to be made. According to Duane Arledge, 50 percent of new church starts don't make it long term. Riverside has seen its share of those, including several failed attempts at starting churches for Gen Xers.

So Riverside has focused on refining the screening process for potential pastors and then mentoring them through the church's Lead Center, which was created to train lay pastors and bi-vocational pastors. Here they are trained in good management practices and group dynamics as well as religious instruction so they are better able to understand the complexity of starting and maintaining a church.

finances, mentoring, and encouragment," says Duane Arledge, who oversees church planting. "They don't have to do their own bookkeeping or deal with administrative stuff. All they have to do is minister. When a guy comes to us with a core group of people ready to start a church, he doesn't also have to know tax laws. But we have to be careful and not get into numbers or new pelts. We have to do this carefully or they will fail. We had eight failures in six years. Individuals may have the desire, a very deep and sincere desire to start a church, but if we don't provide them with the right kind of leadership training, we're headed for trouble."

On the morning I attend the meeting of the pastors of the satellite churches with Ferguson and Arledge, leadership is very much in the forefront. These monthly meetings comprise a continuing course at Riverside. A worksheet ("Organization Paradigm for High Impact Ministry") asks questions such as "What drives an organization?" and pits a policy-driven leadership style against a people-driven model and requires these fledging pastors to fill in the blanks. As they do, they learn once again that it is all about team building and not autocratic dictates, listening not telling, being servants not masters. High relationship and low institutional levels.

While some of the Riverside satellite churches were formed primarily to serve a geographic area, such as a suburb of Denver, many of the congregations are made up of people who share a nationality or culture. "We've been doing this in foreign missions for years," Duane Arledge says. "Finding pockets of people and finding what their culture is."

Friday nights at Riverside probably provide the best picture of exactly how this philosophy of church formation works. Outside Riverside's chapel, rows of Harley-Davidsons are parked in the special "motorcycle parking" area of the church parking lot, and the smell of cigarette smoke lingers in the cool Colorado night air. Inside, Church in the Wind, a church that has evolved from Riverside's outreach to bikers, will meet. "A church might have its token biker," Duane says. "We have a whole community and these are real bikers—grubby jeans and leather. Pastor Gary Davis—I don't think he owns a suit."

And the service, to most seasoned churchgoers, might appear irreverent. But this is where Riverside's theory of repackaging the gospel to make it appealing to different cultures works. Most bikers, according to Gary and Diana Davis, the pastor and his wife, who are bikers themselves, have no formal religious experience and would feel uncomfortable in most churches. They love seventies rock and roll and bluegrass, and many of them have no interest in wearing anything other than jeans, boots, and "rags," or leather vests, many of which have the patch of their motorcycle club sewn on the back. But these read "Christian Riders" or "Christian Motorcyclists Association" rather than "Sons of Silence" or "Banditos." Many of the bikers are, in a sense, prodigal sons and daughters, having left lives of drugs, easy sex, and drinking behind when they became Christians. Most have dramatic stories of conversion, such as Gene Montoya, who was once jobless, addicted to heroin, and living on the streets. He now writes songs and leads worship for Church in the Wind services. "We have a church full of walking miracles," Diana says.

Their worship is heavy on guitars and sounds more like a Rod Stewart concert than a standard church service. Their lyrics tell of their lives: "We are the warriors of the Lord / Sons of thunder on the road / On that straight highway / We will run and give glory to the Son." "Amazing Grace" is sung to the tune of "House of the Rising Sun," which The Animals made popular in the mid-1960s. Because most of the congregation members don't have the formality that is often endemic in church-raised people, they readily and easily raise their hands in the air and close their eyes during worship. At the service researcher Marty Minchin attended, several women wearing long, flowing skirts danced in an ersatz chorus line to the side of the congregation. It was clear they were truly worshiping a God who had changed them and worked in their lives.

"Church in the Wind is a perfect case of contextualizing the gospel," observes Arledge. "Those songs, those melodies ring a bell inside them, they provide a piece of Velcro to attach their spiritual lives. You don't need brick and white columns. They talk about having a service on a Sunday morning inside a country and western bar. That would be perfect—the space is both familiar and, Lord knows, available at that hour." Other satellite churches meet in a truck stop and an apartment complex clubhouse, so a bar wouldn't be such a reach.

And, for the bikers, this is not merely a once a week service. When bikers want to be married or when one of them "goes down," either an accident or death, "Reverend Gorilla" —Gary Davis's CB handle—gets the call. He is their pastor for counseling, personal problems, and life cycle events.

"Riverside gave us the financial support and accountability that we'd been praying for with other churches but we didn't get," Diana says. "At Riverside, someone called us every two weeks to pray with us. Gary and I were blown away that somebody cared. There are people here who are real and who understand."

"I think the key is that we've got to get out of the way of what God wants to do," says Ferguson. "I think too often we try to box God in with the standardized, traditional way of doing church. As long as they come to Christ, what difference do all the trappings make?"

"Getting out of the way" is, of course, not as easy as it sounds. Often the church must follow the lead of the Holy Spirit into places where it has seemingly little in common. Although most of the Riverside congregation is white and middle class, the church decided seven years ago that it should stay in its location in Denver's inner city, even though churches like this often leave the city and move to the suburbs. In Riverside's case, that was certainly tempting. Many of the church's members live in the suburbs, where land is more plentiful and would give the burgeoning church room

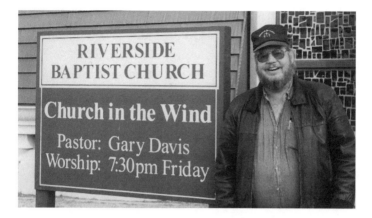

Biker Pastor Gary Davis

to grow. And, as with most white congregations, Pastor Ferguson admits they don't know exactly how to go about ministering to the inner city to which they have committed themselves. "We just pray, and we say, 'Lord, what can we do?' and then a guy like Tad comes along."

Tad Trapp, fresh out of seminary, believed that God was calling him to work with the hardened, homeless teenagers who congregate at Denver's well-known Sixteenth Street Mall. After moving to Denver with his wife and three young children, he spent days hanging out with the teenagers and eventually got to know some of them. One, then two, then three of them became Christians. But, Tad had nowhere to send the new converts. "You lead them to the Lord, and then it's like, 'All right, good luck,'" he says.

After attending Riverside's Sunday service, Tad brought his vision to the pastors, and they agreed to take on a ministry to one of Denver's most difficult demographic groups. "They may not necessarily be experts in the inner city, but they have a passion to do God's will, and this is part of it," Tad says. Standing in the Riverside parking lot, Tad points out a house the church bought and turned into a discipleship home where one of the street kids already lives. Tad, who is now thirty-one, has since seen an outpouring of help from people in the church. One member who's the owner of a multimillion-dollar company has offered to help with the administrative work of the home, and another man who works in construction wants to lend a hand with the renovation of the building. "They're saying, 'Go for it,'" Tad says.

The church has also turned toward the people who live just across the street—hundreds of poor Hispanics, recent immigrants, most of whom arrive in Denver with no job, no money, and no knowledge of English. In 1994, Pastor Richard Vera, a seasoned church planter who lived in Texas, met Rick Ferguson at a conference. "He told me about what was happening in Denver, his vision of a new kind of church and, well, it just happened," Richard says. Six years later, he now leads a Spanish service on Sunday mornings in Riverside's family life center, and his Emmanuel Church, an English service for Hispanic people, has almost two hundred members. Second- and third-generation English-speaking Hispanic people, while well-integrated into American life, often prefer the worship styles of their native culture, so the music has a salsa and mestizo flair.

Although the Spanish service remains small because of the transitory nature of its immigrant population, the church is committed to continuing the service and ministering to the people in the neighborhood. "With a lot of the immigrants, their bodies are here, but their hearts are back in their home-land," Richard Vera says. "We need to keep in mind that we are preparing them for missionary evangelism. We are evangelizing this pocket of people with the understanding that they will be our missionaries when they are deported or they return home. But oftentimes, that does not start with a great sermon or an altar call—it begins with providing the most basic needs of food and clothing."

The church has used events like a weekly tutoring program for children, annual coat and school supplies giveaways, community Thanksgiving dinners, and Christmas toy collections as a bridge to invite the Hispanic people to a church they would normally avoid—a white, Protestant institution. Immigrants also meet church members one-on-one at La Casita Roja, a house across from the church where newly arrived immigrants can get food and clothing while they look for a job. Bill Winter, the executive director of the church's Open Arms ministry, tirelessly collects excess food from such outlets as Safeway, Pizza Hut, and Denny's every week, and volunteers from the church prepare it for distribution. Volunteers also are renovating a house down the street for a crisis pregnancy center. "When my wife and I were introduced as new staff members and mentioned that maybe we would even like to start a crisis pregnancy center, those three words produced an explosive groundswell of interest and support," says Winter. "One woman grabbed me by the arm after the meeting and wouldn't let go until we got into the foyer and she told me how God had given her a vision to do exactly what we were doing."

But beneath the outpouring of Riverside ministries into the neighborhood is the assumption that the aid doesn't end when people are clothed and fed. "Our philosophy is to minister to hurting people in a nonthreatening way and then love them through that process and share the gospel with them because that's where the real solution is," Bill Winter says. He describes one Hispanic couple in their fifties who became Christians after talking and praying with Naomi Gallegos, the former director of La Casita Roja, who worked at a desk by the door. "A few days later the couple came back to the little red house and their skin glowed; the way they dressed was different, and their hygiene was different," Bill says. "Something genuine had happened, and you could see it in their countenances."

Before Rick Ferguson's arrival in 1991, Riverside Baptist Church, like many downtown churches built decades before in a once-affluent, but now deteriorating part of a city, was on the brink of closing. A very public split within the church left it with no staff or pastor, as well as a horrible reputation, and the once-thriving congregation of more than 1,200 was down to about 350, mostly elderly people. At his first meeting of the local ministerial group, one pastor leaned over to Rick and said, "You better be as mean as a junkyard dog if you're going to pastor Riverside."

Ferguson, who is now forty-three years old and who left a conservative, comfortable, suburban St. Louis pastorship to come to Denver, realizes that he had been preparing for such a challenge, but not in the usual way. That bleeding ulcer that had almost destroyed his health and forced him to leave the ministry was his Road to Emmaus experience. "I'd gone through a period of real brokenness before coming here to Denver," he says. "I think the Lord used that, frankly, to teach me dependence on him. I was pretty popular, meeting people's expectations; they applauded. That's pretty intoxicating. But I was pretty hollow inside. My prayer life was mechanical. I was going through a lot of motions to look like a man of God, but there was a lot of 'I' and not enough 'Him.' I realized that you don't grow a church. The Lord is the one who has to do it. It just moved me to a new level of understanding. At the same time He was taking Riverside through a period of brokenness. Maybe He was preparing both of us in that sense."

Riverside now has some three thousand members, a turnaround that can surely be attributed to Ferguson's faith—and his willingness to embrace change and to experiment. "You just can't take a Bible Belt church style and transplant it to Denver. It doesn't work here. It's my contention that churches in the postmodern era can be evangelical but they must appeal to rational apologetics and not only emotional revivalism. That does not last or work for a lot of people."

But longtime members say they stayed with Riverside because of the strong biblical preaching, an area Ferguson will not water down to attract new people. Most of the church's membership has joined in the past six years, and while they also praised the straightforward, hard-hitting preaching, many also say that they have found a way to turn their faith into tangible ministry at Riverside.

On a Friday afternoon several elderly men stuff inserts into that week's church program, a painfully slow job for some because of their shaking hands. "You get old and can't do as many things," says Harley Mullins, who is in his eighties. "There are a lot of things I can't do. I can't run a computer. But this, this I can," he says confidently. On Sunday morning, phone intercessors take calls from people watching the TV broadcast of Riverside's service who want prayer or more information about the free book or tape the church offers at the end of the program. That often leads to conversations about God, giving the phone intercessors an opportunity to witness to people.

Some respond to Riverside's call to live their faith freely and openly. They say the church is their support group, the place where they had found close friends in a city where most people are new, and many transient. Brenda Pierce, forty, answering phones in the church receptionist's office, is misty-eyed as she tells how her life has changed since joining Riverside's 140-member choir. "I visited a lot of different churches," she says. "This is the one where I felt most at home and had ministries I could get involved in. Other than my job, this is where I put my energy. Coming from a conservative, legalistic Baptist background, I'm just amazed at how different worship is here than the church that I grew up in. It's been very freeing to be here and really learn what worship is."

For Stanley Pouw, who had an enormously successful architectural practice but a shattered personal life, Riverside has provided a calm place on life's stormy seas. "I was unfaithful to my wife, my son was in trouble at school, and all I was into was bigger, better, more. The more I accomplished, the worse I felt; I knew I was missing something crucial in my life." Pouw, who was raised in a Christian home in his native Indonesia, admits to being "a typical, stoic Asian guy, one who never said he was wrong, who could never say he was sorry and kept on doing the same things that made him more and more unhappy." Finally, his wife divorced him. Within four months, he lost his business.

A visit from an acquaintance who felt called to pray with him brought Stanley literally and figuratively to his knees. After a marathon reading of the Bible, he came to the conclusion that he must not only ask his ex-wife for forgiveness, but that he should ask her to marry him—again. They courted and remarried and, while looking for a church, visited Riverside. The rest of the pieces fell into place. Stanley's career is on a slower track now, he has a good relationship with his wife and children, and they are the nucleus of a growing Indonesian congregation. "The thing about Riverside is that it just sort of sweeps you in. Everything seems possible here."

A Wednesday evening at the church is typical of Riverside's wonderfully diverse and charismatic presence in people's lives. The place is a virtual beehive of activity, beginning with a meal so that people can come here right from work and

✦ 2. Worship is their "Front Door" ✦

While most of the pastoral staff comes from conservative Midwest Baptist backgrounds, Riverside's pastor and music minister became convinced by reading and studying scripture that the only way for the congregation to understand and practice "making a joyful noise" was if the leaders also practiced it. Rick Ferguson started raising his hands and closing his eyes during worship, and Joel Allen became a much more innovative choir director. He has also turned choir practice into a mini–church service, so that their weekday spirit will infuse the congregation on Sunday morning. "You have to take some chances," says Allen, "but if you feel it, do it and people will follow, gladly." Riverside's Sunday service has an orchestra section, with drums, guitars, and brass instruments, that plays more praise choruses than hymns. Choir members close their eyes, sway back and forth, and raise their hands, motions that are mirrored in both the congregation and worship leaders.

take part in activities. There is a parenting group, a youth Bible study, and a Hispanic group meeting. But most interesting is Evangelism 101, a course that 800 people have signed up for. This Wednesday about 120 gather in a large meeting room for a PowerPoint presentation of how to—nonthreateningly—spread the good news. From how to break the ice when talking about religion to the point of inviting someone to Riverside, the succinct, hour-long presentation is a model of both efficiency and efficacy.

As many students of congregational life and church growth will point out, rarely is there a thriving church nowadays without a thriving worship life, and Riverside has acknowledged that many younger people no longer connect with the hymns of the eighteenth and nineteenth centuries that many churches use week after week. The transition to a freer, more spirit-filled service began several years ago at the Southern Baptist Convention, where the Riverside choir was leading worship. Ferguson felt a twinge, an inner prodding to raise his hands to God during the singing. But he admits he was afraid of what the other pastors would think, so he kept his hands rigidly at his side.

But the twinge was not a passing one. Convinced that he should have followed that feeling, upon returning to Riverside Rick confessed the incident to his congregation and preached a series of sermons on biblical worship. He found that in the Bible it was not uncommon for people to dance and clap during worship.

Now, a Sunday morning at Riverside looks a lot more like a place where the singing, dancing, clapping King David of the Psalms would fit in. Choir director Joel Allen bobs up and down, leans side-to-side, and waves his arms in huge arcs as he conducts. Rick claps or stands, eyes closed and arms raised, as he sings. In the congregation, there is none of the regimented sitting and standing common in traditional churches. People sit or stand as they wish, some with eyes shut and faces and arms raised, others with heads bowed in a prayerful posture.

Joel Allen believes that the transformation in worship at Riverside could not have been done without consensus and conviction among the church leaders that they wanted to worship like this. Rick and Joel have become the best of friends, a relationship Joel says is essential to worship. "It's hard to lead worship when you're on the platform with someone you hardly know," Joel says. Their close friendship is also easily evident to the congregation, who are often privy to the pair's fishing rivalry when—between screen changes on the Jumbotron on each side of the choir loft where the words to the songs are displayed—up will flash a photo of Joel (or Rick, for that matter) holding a large fish.

To create an authentic, participatory worship at Riverside, Joel has turned Wednesday night choir practice into a mini-church service. He defines the group as a "called choir" rather than a volunteer choir, which means that members are asked to join only if they feel that God is leading them to. With about 140 of the choir's 195 active members attending every week, the group has become like a small family. "I let the choir share what God's doing in their hearts," Joel said. "When you start having people testify about how good God is, you can't help but sing in worship." Joel also instructs the choir to rehearse worship, not music. "I want it to be as musical as it can be, but I want people to see God for who he is, not the music for what it is."

That means involving the congregation in all aspects of worship on Sunday morning. Traditionally, church worship involves hymn singing as well as "special music," such as choir anthems, solos, and pageants at Easter and Christmas. But at Riverside, the congregation is always involved in the singing. During "special music," the words to the songs are flashed on the screens so people can follow, or sing, along. "I don't want the congregation just to watch it happen, I want them to help make it happen," Joel says.

As appealing as their various ministries and those spirit-filled Sunday services are, Riverside is not a church that thinks people will come just by word of mouth or even through the efforts of the Evangelism 101 graduates. They

✦ 3. EFFECTIVE MEDIA; 80 PERCENT COME THIS WAY ✦

Riverside found that 80 percent of their new members get their first contact with the church through some kind of media, so the church utilizes both print advertising and the television and radio broadcasts of Rick's preaching as evangelical tools. Callers are not necessarily encouraged to come to the main church building, but to the Riverside church nearest them. And if they call from outside the Denver area, they will be directed to a church close by. Following up, the intercessor will also call that church to make sure the connection is forged.

have an active and varied communications ministry. But the big difference at Riverside is that this is a church that immediately gets personal. Callers will in turn be called back by a church member who asks if they have needs the church can meet and invites them to a service or activity. And, with all of Riverside's satellite churches in the suburbs, they are also now able to direct callers to a Riverside church plant near them.

Late one night during my Denver visit when I get back to my motel room and open the curtain, there in the distance is the brilliant red Riverside sign, proclaiming that this is a church that indeed is not about to hide its lamp. Denver will have a choice of whether to respond, but Riverside is going to make that call, over and over, biblically sound and culturally astute, in ways mainstream churches might never have thought possible.

6

First United Methodist Church

1008 Eleventh Street
Santa Monica, CA 90403
310-393-8258
www.santamonicaumc.org

✦ POINTS OF EXCELLENCE ✦

1. Leadership—call them by name

2. Small groups, constantly reorganizing

3. Church-government cooperation

It is one of those crystalline mornings in Santa Monica, early enough for pigeons and the homeless to be about their breakfasts, but not yet time for most other inhabitants of this beach outpost of Los Angeles to have risen. It is Sunday, and the benign gaze of the statue of Saint Monica looks impassively up a quiet Wilshire Boulevard as I walk from the ocean where she stands guard to a church —though not exactly in her tradition—but nonetheless an integral part of the religious life of this once sleepy, now quite posh oceanside city.

First United Methodist, Santa Monica, is surely a far cry from the simple gatherings of the poor and downtrodden who flocked to hear the reassuring words of Methodism's founder, John Wesley. For then his message—that God's mercy and love are available to all—was preached to those on the lowest rungs of the social ladder. On the other hand, membership in FUMC, Santa Monica was until quite recently a statement about a sure place in this city's business, professional, and social life.

On this Sunday morning, I am on my way up Wilshire to talk with the pastor of this prestigious church, a pastor who further underscores the changes that have happened both here, in mainstream Protestantism, and within Methodism, which in 1968 joined with the Evangelical United Brethren to form the United Methodist Church. For the world has changed, and changed drastically, since the glory days of First United Methodist, Santa Monica.

The pastor, forty-eight-year-old Patricia Farris, is one of a tiny fraction (some 2 percent) of women ministers who have broken through the glass ceiling to head large mainline churches. But when she arrived at FUMC some two years ago, daunting problems were at hand. She was, of course, a woman and would be replacing a beloved man who was an excellent homilist, sure-handed administrator, and had been in place for twenty-three years. But an even more vexing problem: There was no parking. On the crowded streets of

Blessed, and sent forth

Santa Monica, this is no small matter. The first Methodists might have been eager to hear the hoofbeats of John Wesley's approaching horse, but the hearts of these First United Methodists were not strangely warmed by the honk of the shuttle bus that transported them from a nearby community college parking lot.

"At one time you said, 'I'm a member of First Church' and everyone immediately knew who you were; your place was assured," Patricia Farris says, her signature wide smile spreading across her face. "Because at one time in this city, if you were to be reckoned with and weren't Catholic, you were most likely Methodist and you were a member of First Church. Now you say First Church and someone is as likely to come back that they do crystals or tarot cards."

Elegantly tall, this morning Patricia is wearing a canary yellow blazer. Her flaming red hair catches the early rays of light streaming into the manicured courtyard outside her window. No ministerial grays need apply here.

While the church is still a pillar of Santa Monica with two thousand members, that pillar had begun to erode well before Patricia arrived. But little had been done about it, for

First Church had a reputation for decades as the home of outstanding music and preaching—so much so that in the 1960s the Easter services were held in the Santa Monica Civic Auditorium to accommodate the crowds. But the congregation was so large and so wealthy for so long that the gradual slippage in membership went almost unnoticed. It is an all-too-common problem. Many mainline churches that thrived in the fifties, sixties, and seventies, especially those now with aging, middle- to upper-class congregations, are struggling with similar membership declines.

And so, in addition to the crucial parking problem (which was actually already being addressed) Patricia went to work on what she realized would be a much larger task; completely reorienting the First Church culture. She sensed that this church could easily become still another of the grand old irrelevant relics of American church life if it did not change.

"Yes, some people left when I came, but that always happens when a new pastor arrives," she says. "I was actually surprised there was so little resistance at their new pastor being a woman. What did shock me was how dysfunctional we were as a body. We had so many people in the wrong places. People had forgotten it was their church, not the ministers' church. They were used to decisions being made here (she looks around her neat office) and not by them. It wasn't a case of throwing out everything. We had old wineskins and we needed new wine. What to hold it in? To say it another way, we have excellent traditions in Methodism and in this local church, but needed to approach church life in a new way to confront a culture that robs people of their worth and the sacredness of the presence of God. No longer did mere membership work; we had to rebuild this church from within. We had to learn together how to layer one on top of the other. And I underscore we."

While women have been ordained in increasing numbers in many mainline churches since the 1970s, Patricia Farris in essence represents a second generation. The first were the women pioneers who were praised for their determination to seek orders, but sometimes earned less praise for their single-minded, agenda-driven approach to church life. For them, change was a revolution that had to be staged immediately; the local church often served as a bewildered staging ground.

"I think what impressed us right from the beginning about Patricia was her gentle way of making change," says Mike Olsson, a forty-eight-year-old UCLA administrator. "I'm sure she had firm ideas about what needed to be done, but we never felt that. Decisions were reached because the majority of the people saw them as the right way to go. It's not a gender thing, it's a matter of style: Patricia could set ideas and a vision before us and these became our ideas, our vision. She never rammed anything down our throats and that's why so many people got on board. They were ready for a collaborative ministry and the way Patricia did it was not merely window dressing; we were all in this together and whatever seemed the best path was the one we would take, regardless of whose it was."

And change First United Methodist Patricia Farris did—everything from leadership to liturgy to the building of a labyrinth. Virtually every part of First Church's life has undergone either minor corrections or a sea of changes. Instead of focusing her efforts on increasing membership through impersonal methods such as snazzy mass mailings, phone call canvasses, and advertising, Patricia has focused many of her efforts on "inreach," on the lives of people already attending church, many of them lifelong members. These are in a demographic group that can be extraordinarily difficult to change —people who are economically comfortable, successful, and educated. People who suffer from drug addiction, poverty, or other societal diseases can clearly see a void in their lives, but for those prosperous enough to live in and around Santa Monica, the need for God may be much less apparent. The changes in their lives, when they happen, frequently involve arduous intellectual struggle, and the results can be much more subtle.

Patricia Farris started by simply handing the church back to its people. But there was something far more important than mere institutional restructuring. As member after member told Parish/Congregation researcher Marty Minchin and me on our visits to the church, they have been introduced to a *living* God within these walls and in their lives. A spiritual awakening has begun.

Louana Seibold felt that stirring. Louana, a slight woman with bobbed brown hair who works as a midwife, was born in Santa Monica and grew up in the church's children's and youth programs. But for years, her attendance was just an obligation. "I've always come on Sunday, partly because there was never an excuse not to come. I never really knew why." But once a new kind of pastoral style, which Patricia represented, was in place; it was like a dry layer of the church's soil was raked off to reveal the rich, moist soil of vibrant people ready to claim ownership in the church.

For Louana, who had never held a leadership position in the church, suddenly being in charge of the evangelism committee has forced her to reevaluate the role of evangelism in her own life. In her secular role as a midwife, she now talks more openly with her patients about their spirituality. "The strength of my convictions allows my patients to speak about their convictions," she says. "I challenge members of my committee to actively look for ways to go out into the community." One example of this is the successful church-sponsored

✦ 1. LEADERSHIP—CALL THEM BY NAME ✦

The need for more lay leadership to relieve overburdened staff and prevent laity burnout is a struggle in most churches. Pastor Patricia Farris didn't wait for people to step forward— after years of attending and not volunteering for leadership, why would they now? Instead, she straightforwardly asked certain people she had identified as potential leaders to take on major responsibilities, such as heading up important church committees. "Always be specific—tell people exactly what the need is and what they might contribute," she says. "Most were shocked when they were asked, wondering if they were capable of such leadership. They were."

community softball team, a first for First United Methodist, which in years past might have thought such an activity a bit déclassé. Church facilities are not only for members' use but also for other community groups. "We want to open our doors and tell the community they are welcome here."

Chuck Cole, sixty, was raised in the Methodist Church, but drifted away over the years as he became a highly successful businessman, married, divorced, and remarried. He began attending FUMC about seven years ago because he was looking for a good Christian education for his daughter, who is now fourteen years old. Even though he was an usher in the church, Chuck says his spiritual life was empty during his first few years there.

"Before Patricia arrived at best I could be called a lazy Christian," Chuck says. But hearing him talk now, he is anything but that. He exudes excitement about his involvement in the church and the future growth he envisions because of the changes he's seen in himself and other people in the church. "My spiritual journey picked up pace about a year and a half ago. I listened to her preach and I realized I had a lump in my throat. It was like she was preaching directly to me. And it was funny because quite a few of us felt that way."

If the new Protestant church is really a church of, for, and by the people, finding excellent lay leaders is surely crucial. While First Church could always list an impressive number of its members on this committee or that board, something was missing. While most members adored the former pastor, they often felt they were left out of major church decisions, as if FUMC was *his* church, not *their* church. With Patricia came a new sense of confidence in lay leadership and a feeling of personal ownership.

For those who have responded to Patricia's not-all-that-subtle requests, changes have occurred in both church life and personal lives. "In the old days, if we got five to seven people to show up that would be a good meeting," Chuck says. But now, a condition of being on the committee is a commitment

Dress code: flexible

to attend meetings, and people have responded. "They were just waiting to be asked to do something meaningful for the church. After all, these are people who are used to accomplishing things; they know what that requires."

Most agree that upping their investment in the life of the church has transformed their own relationship with God into something vital and dynamic. "The more you're involved in church life, the more spiritual you are," Chuck says, "the more lively and rich a church you have."

Chuck was a wise choice for finance director of the church. Retired for six years, he began working in the computer industry early in his fifty-year career and successfully stayed on the cutting edge of technology. He was a venture capitalist for start-up technology companies for years, and he also was a professor of business at the University of Southern California. His business know-how transformed the finance committee and revamped the church's finances.

"I joined the finance committee and was absolutely opposed to most of the things they were doing," he says, "so I changed our approach." From dipping into the church's "rainy day pot" to pay for the hiring of two new, young associate pastors to reach neglected segments of the population to instituting the reading of scripture at every committee meeting, members have found a new sense of both pragmatic and spiritual purpose.

But even more significant have been the changes in Chuck's own life, changes that are mirrored in other former lukewarm churchgoers. "I think I've become more tolerant, more patient, and I spend a lot of time reading the Bible," he said. "I'm not stuck on it and I don't stop people on street corners, but I want to do more good things with my life."

To Claudia Flanders's utter amazement, Patricia asked her, one of the behind-the-scenes stalwarts who had led classes from kindergarten age to UCLA college students, to act as chairwoman of the church council. She was given the mandate to change the structure and nature of the committee. Claudia, like Louana, grew up at First Church, but not until she became head of the church council did she really see a spiritual change in herself. "Patricia afforded me something I strangely never experienced at the church: trust and understanding," Claudia says. "Before, it was, 'We've never done it that way,' so we didn't. Now we go where it makes sense."

In her own life, Claudia has found herself more connected to God. When she asked committee chairmen to bring Bible passages about hospitality—a practice Patricia has stressed since she arrived—to the meetings, Claudia also had to read the Bible to find verses herself. "I began to read passages of the Bible I'd never really reflected on and read before," she says. She has also felt compelled to live out what she's reading. Where she once would have not paid much attention to church visitors, she now finds herself approaching new people at the coffee hour fellowship between Sunday services and engaging them in conversation. "It's made me a much more responsible Christian."

Small groups—the key to many church renewals—had been started by an associate minister, Se Hee Han, but they matured further after Patricia arrived. She encouraged not their permanence, but their transience.

And while local churches sometimes view denomination-wide programs warily, Patricia readily embraced "Together in Christ," an intensive, nine-month course in prayer, study, and discernment. "It is not a direct answer to remedy a specific situation," she says, "but exactly the kind of a considered approach that will give people both the knowledge and the tools for a fuller faith life."

One of the members of that group is forty-seven-year-old

✦ 2. SMALL GROUPS, CONSTANTLY
REORGANIZING ✦

While some churches pride themselves on small Christian communities that have stayed together for years, at First Church individuals are encouraged to move from group to group. In essence, small communities are continually broken up and reconstituted, depending on personal interest. "In a large congregation, focus can change, different issues can come up," says member Mary Lois Roney. "A group might want to focus on political issues or homosexuality or spirituality, so to us it makes sense for members to constantly reevaluate the group and their role in it. I think it also helps us not to be too insular, too comfortable with our little circle of friends."

Nancy Scharfenaker. Nancy moved seven times before she was nine years old and went to whatever church was close by. "It was more like enrolling for school in a new town than having any connection with God," she says. She drifted away from church entirely as she grew older, "but I kept meeting people, happy people who really believed in God and had a church home." The mother of a Chinese infant she and her husband, Chris, adopted, Nancy found Santa Monica a lonely place for an at-home mother of an infant. The idea of looking for a church home for herself cropped up, but she didn't know how to go about it. "What do you do? Where to go? How to act? When do I stand and when do I sit down? What prayers did I need to know?"

The tragic death of a friend in an automobile accident coupled with a chance conversation with another mom at the

YMCA led her to First Church. She cried the first Sunday and most every other Sunday she attended for the first year and decided she had to find out what her tears were about. She signed up for "Together in Christ," which required a two-hour commitment each Wednesday evening.

"My old approach was that we are born alone, live alone, die alone," she says. "That changed when I began to really read the Bible, when I opened my heart to God and to the people in that group. Now, I say: How can people *not* believe in God? We're hardly perfect, but someone is always there for us. We're never alone, even when we choose to be. He's always there. Patricia, who led the course, really helped me see that."

After graduating from Harvard Divinity School, Patricia Farris held a series of successful pastorates even though, she admits, "My husband and I are a little odd, not exactly the typical ministerial profile. We have different last names (his name is David Bremer), no kids, and he doesn't work in the church." But her warmth and pastoral acuity meant more than having that classic profile—married, with kids—and she was eventually named one of the few women district superintendents in the United Methodist Church. Accountable for forty-eight churches in a two-county area, she was viewed as an up-and-coming leader. Each Sunday she worshiped at a different church, at each stop displaying that winning smile, words of encouragement, and guidance.

But there was more to it than that. She found she had inherited a senior pastor, beloved by his congregation, but who had been systematically sexually abusing female members and staff. "When nobody likes you for what you are doing—for what I had to do in that man's case—you have to find another grounding, a grounding that goes beyond the institution, to God, to the deepest part of you, to what you really believe in. That experience toughened me and it took a toll."

Beyond the agony and the occasional ecstasy of being a district superintendent, Patricia missed daily contact with a congregation, "that humbling realization that people trust you with themselves." So when she was offered the position at First Church, she put that part of her promising career on hold and leaped at the chance.

Whenever anyone inside or outside her church compliments the progress First Church has made, Patricia is quick to say that this is a work in progress, that renewal has just begun at this venerable church. A compassionate, process-oriented, consensus-building pastor doesn't turn the tide overnight, but Patricia's two years at First Church have seen many more women (and a sprinkling of men) coming forward to lay down their burdens and ask this living God to enter their lives.

This is a church transforming itself from the inside out, and not in flashy, horn-blowing ways, but with a leadership style driven by decidedly feminine traits (a style not necessarily genetically limited to women, but women seem to display it more often than their male counterparts) that is bringing about quiet, deep, and powerful changes. Membership at First Church hasn't risen dramatically, although attendance at Sunday worship (a phenomenon that is evident in other excellent mainline churches) is up.

That Sunday worship is a combination of old elegance (a regal procession of children and burgundy-robed choir members, the sound of a magnificent Turner organ) and new openness (there are both suits and shorts in the pews and the Lord's Prayer is printed in the bulletin for the uninitiated). And Patricia, who is careful about both that old wineskin and fermenting the new wine, has brought back the liturgical seasons to the church while presiding with a certain relaxed, almost youthful enthusiasm. On the Pentecost Sunday I am in

Santa Monica, she senses the nine o'clock service is going on too long and sets aside her prepared homily to harken back to the FUD (fear, uncertainty, and doubt) the disciples felt on their Pentecost day. "Here at First Methodist, where spontaneity is rare, let's feel that fire, feel that wind. The disciples were huddled in their room too and they didn't want to go out. We have to take what we have felt here into the world."

"How to assess what is happening? I would say it's a church where the level of positive emotion is rising," says Mike Olsson. In a city of boutique bottled water and goat cheese–arugula salads, members say they want more old-fashioned covered-dish dinners: Jell-O salads and meatloaf. "This is an upscale city on the surface, but just beneath are ordinary people who want to break out of their cocoons of home, car, and job and find some honest community," says Nancy Scharfenaker.

That the culture at First United Methodist will be continually challenged to change is symbolized by the building across the street, its brainchild and yet not its possession. While the church gives almost $250,000 a year to global missions and regularly receives plaques from the Westside Food Bank as its most generous annual donor, taking care of people who walk right by the front door is something the church wanted to address. First United Methodist prayed and thought about and discussed what the community needs were: affordable housing for senior citizens who were being driven from the community by spiraling housing costs and shelter for the many homeless who gravitate to Santa Monica because of the mild weather.

The question of whether both of these needs might be met in a single structure was one part of the equation, but there was an even larger issue. In this somewhat government-adverse community, the reality set in: If such a structure were

✦ 3. CHURCH—GOVERNMENT
COOPERATION ✦

When First Church learned the project it had in mind would cost $17 million, church organizers turned to HUD and numerous other agencies that had similar—though secular—goals. "The church had resources, it had land," says Andrew Parker, executive director of Upward Bound House, the non-profit agency that oversees Senior Villa and Family Place. It also had other capital, a presence in the community, and, as churches are establishing themselves as reliable partners, government agencies are more and more willing to enter into these partnerships. Certain members of the church were opposed not only to the partnership but also to the use of land and funds that had been left to the church, ostensibly for exclusively church purposes. "But unless churches see beyond their walls, we're all missing the point," says Patricia Farris.

to be built, federal, state, and city money would be required. And secular, not religious, standards would be imposed. In other words, First Methodist senior members would have to apply like everyone else. And so, the church's parking lot across the street was torn up and an underground parking deck dug beneath what would become Family Place, transitional housing for the homeless, as well as Senior Villa, in another part of the new structure, which would be called Upward Bound House.

Coalitions in other communities have shown that one way for churches to bring about significant social change is to stop seeing themselves as islands and to start working with other churches and social justice agencies. Faith-based substance abuse programs have often proved more effective than government social programs and as a result, more government money is becoming available.

The Family Place program is already a success. There, homeless people are moved into a more stable environment and offered job training and counseling services. So far, the program has had thirty-five graduates. "There are incredible stories of hardships people have overcome," Patricia says. "When somebody believes in them it makes all the difference."

First Church's project is a good example of a collaborative effort between church and state. The Upward Bound office and its staff work out of the second floor of the church office building, yet its advisory board is drawn from the community at large, regardless of religious affiliation or lack of one. When the agency needed programs for the older children whose parents lived in Family Place, instead of starting from scratch and creating their own, they sent the children to the Boys and Girls clubs already established in Santa Monica.

Now the church is tackling a bigger obstacle: trying to make connections between its members and the people living in Senior Villa and Family Place. Patricia admits that there are awkward social differences between many of the people who volunteer and the residents. Some church members have also been upset that because Senior Villa was financed in part by HUD, residents for the sixty-nine units were chosen from a lottery of two thousand applicants, and only one church member won a spot.

But, as Patricia states, "although it's right across the street, it really is clearly about mission outreach." Executive director Andrew Parker and his staff are planning intergenerational programs where the seniors will spend time with the children in Family Place. "We strongly believe there has to be some common ground between the families at one facility and the seniors at the other facility," Andrew says. The church is also turning to people in the congregation to volunteer to tutor and serve as mentors for the children.

Yes, like all of the excellent churches the Parish/Congregation Study discovered, First United Methodist, Santa Monica, is a work in progress. The youth group still attracts good, but mostly churchy, kids and teenage visitors often come once and then go. Hospitality is stressed in many meetings, but it is a difficult concept to put into practice, as Americans continue to live in the cocoons Nancy Scharfenaker talks about. Seniors and the homeless at Upward Bound have still not formed a cooperative community the church once envisioned.

But Saint Monica looks on, serene from her beachside vantagepoint as the echoes of John Wesley's horse sound through the fine streets of Santa Monica. Something is happening at First Church and each of them—along with a pastor and her people—must feel somewhat responsible.

7

Chinese Christian Union Church

2301 South Wentworth Avenue
Chicago, IL 60616
312- 842-8545
www.ccuc.net

✦ POINTS OF EXCELLENCE ✦

1. Pre-evangelization

2. Homogeneous groupings; if people are not comfortable, they don't come

3. Lay involvement: matching needs with faces

For a church with an activities center that was once a notorious gambling den, the Chinese Christian Union Church might seem to possess far too checkered a past and an uncertain future for growth.

Great expectations

But, set as it is in the middle of Chicago's bustling Chinatown —at once steeped in Chinese culture, but informed by Christian teachings—it has defied popular wisdom. CCUC has proved to be that rare Asian church that has managed to serve a continuing stream of recent immigrants while holding on to those who have moved into America's mainstream. It has found new ways to reach that crucial and most difficult group —the ABCs, American-born children of foreign-born Chinese who are often whipsawed between the ancient values of their forebears and the siren call of American trendiness and commercialism. For all of these groups and ages, CCUC has squarely recognized and honored the pull of ancient Chinese culture. But when Chinese and Christian ways are in conflict, they have intelligently offered the good news as a life-giving, sustaining force in people's lives.

While many churches that serve immigrant congregations often stall in the missionary mode that has worked so well for so many decades—stylized evangelization, stiff foreign-language services, church boards dominated by elderly foreign-speaking members—Chinese Christian Union Church has adapted, both to the changing needs of vastly different kinds of Chinese who have come to America and to a church landscape that is being reshaped by innovative approaches to liturgy and evangelization. With its emphasis on relevant liturgies to meet Americanized taste, yet a commitment to the person who has just arrived from China, speaks no English, and for whom God may never have even been a consideration, CCUC is a rich amalgam of superchurch methods coupled with a Jane Addams–settlement house approach.

"We have great dreams," says Key Wong, a twenty-eight-year-old layman and the church's business manager. Seated at a computer in his cramped office just off a busy reception area that is open from morning until late into the night, he is no more than five feet from the busy Wentworth Avenue sidewalk. Key is one of the CCUC lay people who is defying the old model of ethnic ministers and setting the tone for a church that sees to the needs of a congregation that ranges from kitchen workers in Chicago's five hundred Chinese restaurants to Ph.D.'s at prestigious biotech firms. "We are growing in size, yes," he says in his quiet voice. "But," he adds with typical Chinese modesty, "we hope to also grow in maturity, not just numbers."

Chinese Christian Union Church's history is a rich and fascinating one. Started in 1915 by a consortium of Protestant denominations—Methodist, Congregational, Presbyterian, Baptist, and Disciples of Christ—to serve Chinese immigrants, the church became independent by the mid-1940s. "In those days, there was terrible discrimination," says Stephen Yeh Sr., who has been a church member for more than fifty years. "We were all poor and the collection was maybe four or five dollars a week, but we wanted a place where we could worship God in peace and not be called all sorts of names. No churches wanted us."

The church moved several times until it found a home on Wentworth Avenue and Twenty-third Street. But with a growing congregation, space was always a problem in this crowded, commercial area. When U.S. Marshals broke down the doors of the architecturally gorgeous but quite notorious building owned by the On Leong Merchants Association, CCUC looked down Wentworth Avenue with hope. The building, which had once served as Chinatown's unofficial town hall with its own courts and counselors to address everything from abusive husbands to bad debts, had been degraded into little more than a gambling den. Perhaps the church could buy it?

Over the years, the church had served thousands who had come from mainland China—many of them poor, illiterate, rural peasants, and then came the exodus of the intelligentsia forced out by Mao Tse-tung's revolution and the establishment of Chiang Kai-shek's government on Taiwan. While the Cantonese-speaking Taiwanese continued to emigrate to the United States, a new kind of immigrant followed after President Nixon helped open Red China to the world in 1972. These were China's top students: young, often unmarried, Mandarin-speaking, and most of them thoroughly indoctrinated and believing that any kind of religion was only for the weak and stupid. Mao had convinced them that their brainpower and loyalty to Red China was all they needed for happy, fruitful lives.

By the mid-1990s, two things were happening at CCUC. The first was that it had begun to discover and perfect a three-pronged approach: pre-evangelization, evangelization, and spiritual growth. Each step required not only different approaches but different languages—Mandarin, Cantonese, and English—to reach each language group. The second was that if the church was to grow and meet those needs, in addition to its social service outreach, either it had to move— which would end its mission here at the heart of the Chinese community—or it would have to expand.

Mr. Yeh, who came to America a penniless peasant and built a sizable shoe-importing business, was the chairman of the church board when he set his sights on the old gambling den, which sat vacant and litter-strewn for five years as the American courts dealt with the club's owners. He went to city hall, and he visited Illinois senator Paul Simon to plead his case. When the church's offer for the building fell short of a higher bid, he called on the U.S. Marshal in charge of the building. "He was a Catholic, so I knew I could approach him on religious grounds," says Mr. Yeh, an eighty-two-year-old in a dark suit and crisp white shirt, who carries himself with regal bearing. "We wanted to serve God and serve this neighborhood, I told him." His persistence and obvious sincerity won out.

The church renovated the building and gave it the decidedly secular name of the Pui Tak Center, which roughly translated means "cultivating virtue." "And who can be against cultivating virtue, whatever their experience has been with religion?" asks David Wu, the center's executive director. "Our purpose was not to blare out to the world that this was a quote unquote 'Christian' place. Rather, we wanted people to see it as a safe haven, a place that welcomed them, met their needs."

Pui Tak was perfectly in keeping with the first of the three stages that Chinese Christian Union saw as its mission: something the church calls "pre-evangelization." Although the church had maintained a nursery for more than forty years and had provided language and citizenship classes, the center allowed it to both expand those classes and move them out of the crowded main building, which housed a sanctuary, gym, offices, and classrooms.

"We want people to be attracted to this church because of what we do, not what we say," says Rev. John Chao, who heads the Mandarin-speaking congregation. "We always have

✦ 1. PRE-EVANGELIZATION ✦

Pre-evangelization is at the heart of CCUC's work. A lavish Thanksgiving meal attracts hundreds of non-Christian students from area colleges such as the University of Illinois-Chicago for whom this American holiday is just another reminder of how far away from home and family they are. A Chinese New Year's party draws hundreds more. Strategically placed at the table are members of the church who, while not doing this in a heavy-handed manner, offer testimony to what CCUC and Christianity has meant in their lives. English and citizenship classes are offered to anyone who wants to come —and this past fall five hundred signed up for classes. Welcome boxes containing both personal items, guides to services, and church literature are distributed to all new immigrants. A nursery is available for working parents, and there is also a medical clinic. All this is done without any quid pro quo about church attendance or membership.

to remind ourselves that for those who came from the mainland God was so much foolishness, if they had even heard about God. For many of them, God wasn't even on the screen. There is what we call a 'vacuum of truth.' They are under tremendous strain; there is tremendous pressure on the family. They must excel in their studies, or they will have to go back. For the less educated Chinese who come, they might be picked up for work at ten in the morning and not get home until midnight. We want to extend a hand of friendship and the best time to do this is in their first year here, when their needs are the greatest."

At CCUC, it is called "friendship evangelism," simply meeting the immediate need for people—whether it be the gateway to this strange English language of ours; care for the children of struggling immigrant couples, both of whom may be working in restaurants; a gym where a good game of volleyball is exactly what is required after a tough day at work or in the classroom; or a nonthreatening bookstore with books and tapes in a language they understand. And this "friendship evangelization" goes the extra step, not just with a class or facilities, but by becoming involved in people's lives, seeing them not just as potential converts, but as human beings in need.

Each form of pre-evangelization at CCUC implants the memory of the church in a person's heart. Many never become Christians; but they never forget who was there for them when they needed it the most. But many do choose to become a part of what they discover is an attractive, appealing way of living; the stories of conversion at CCUC abound.

In Rosanna Ng's cheery bookstore on the ground floor of the Pui Tak Center, the offerings are clearly Christian, although there is no sign outside advertising that it's a Christian bookstore. "We want to allow people to be convinced that Christianity is good for them. People say China is a godless place. My answer is that when God created every person, he put something in him or her that cannot be reached by anything other than a relationship with him. We want to take people on the steps to that relationship and these books, these tapes, the way we greet them, all can contribute to that."

She points to a place just behind a high display of books where a Cantonese-speaking man, recently arrived from Taiwan, had a life-changing experience. "He was living with a woman, they were not married, working horrible hours at restaurants, arguing all the time. The woman began coming to church and Bible study and she changed. He saw what a

✦ 2. HOMOGENEOUS GROUPINGS; IF PEOPLE ARE NOT COMFORTABLE, THEY DON'T COME ✦

"While it might seem like the ideal to have the entire congregation together, for us it just doesn't work," says Rev. John Chao. "If people do not feel comfortable in their surroundings and with the service, they don't come." CCUC has the additional problem of space, not having a worship area big enough to hold the nine hundred people who come on an average Sunday. "Even if we had a huge sanctuary, these smaller services really fit people's needs better. Language is one thing, but the liturgical approach is another. One size fits all isn't the case with churches anymore. Having a full house is good, but if a service becomes too crowded, that is also another turnoff. We are always conscious of allowing people to have enough room and the type of service that works for them."

difference this could make in her life and one day, right there, he went down on his knees and accepted Christ. They eventually got married and now they have a much better life."

Through their numerous activities and outreach, CCUC has attracted many Chinese immigrants and, while not pressing church attendance on anyone who comes to them for help or comradeship, the invitation to attend one of the worship services is continually extended. As they are offered in Cantonese, Mandarin, and English, language cannot be considered a barrier.

"I think where we are different," says senior pastor Rev. Michael Tsang, "is that we have both activities and services in all three languages. We are trying to reach the entire family. While they may be speaking different languages in their lives —their children learning in English, for instance—that is no reason for them to have to go to different places for their Christian training and worship."

The three services held on Sunday mornings (there is also a Monday morning service for restaurant workers) both in the Pui Tak Center and in the main sanctuary, which was once a Catholic church, are emblematic of the diverse approaches the church uses. The Mandarin service at 9:45 (150 attending) and the Cantonese service at 11:00 (400) have a more traditional feel to them, keeping with the temperaments of older congregants. But the English service at 9:45 (350) has a contemporary approach and attracts both younger members, their parents, and those who are more comfortable with the language.

On the Sunday I attend, Mike Wang begins by leading his five-piece band (two guitars, two female singers, and drums) through a series of modern hymns whose words are projected on the front wall. This twenty-six-year-old computer programmer would have been the last person to be thought worthy—or who could have demanded attention of churchgoers—not that many years ago. But there he is, at ease with spontaneous prayer, with a rich voice—a comfortable yet commanding presence with his guitar strapped over his shoulder. Interspersed with the songs are short meditations. "What's on your mind this morning?" "How are you dealing with the issues and problems in your life?" "Where are you drawing strength?" The reassuring words of Psalm 31 ("In you, O Lord, I take refuge") offer an answer.

A sheet in the Sunday bulletin asks some open-ended questions, such as, "What battles are you fighting today?" The printed answers have blanks for congregants to fill in: "The Lord fights for those who _____."

When the time for the sermon is at hand, another young face appears in the pulpit. Rev. Donald Moy, who usually leads and preaches for the English-speaking service, is away, but Mike Gin fills in seamlessly with a powerful sermon based on Joshua 10:40–42 entitled "Successful Living: The Ultimate Secret Weapon." He stands to the side of a stark, gold-painted cross flanked by two faux stained-glass panels and recalls that Joshua's ragtag army ultimately prevailed because God was on their side. "And you?" he asks.

Before him are those young people who in other Asian churches have been part of what is called the "silent exodus." Once there is no longer any enforcement of the mandatory church attendance of their early years, they simply drift away from churches that do not provide a worship experience or activities that resonate with them.

It is typical of CCUC that those with "Rev." before their names are not always the moving force or the public face of this dynamic church. A second echelon of lay leaders, both younger members like Key Wong and senior ones like Mr. Yeh, as well as seminarians like Mike Gin or those who feel called to minister but have not attended a seminary, are the true driving force in this church. "The pastors are the shepherds," says Key, "but we are the small-group leaders, we are the ones who can mobilize others to take belief into their lives."

Having people make the decision to become Christians is important, to be sure, in all churches, but equally important at Chinese Christian Union is what happens after that decision is made. "We cannot just have Christians in name!" says Rev. John Chao, the Mandarin congregation's voluble pastor. "Our work has just begun when that happens; then we have to deepen that faith and show people how they take it into their lives. And remember, our congregation ranges from people who have never so much as heard of

God (God is love? Who is God?) to those who know him as Savior.

"By and large the Mandarin-speaking are very intelligent, the top one percent or else they would have never been sent to the United States for study. So we cannot just say 'believe' and expect them to believe. They are seeking truth, but they will not accept easy, simplistic answers. Yes, they know they are finally free when they arrive in America, but they are still starving for the real truths of life, which have been denied them by a government that told them religion was only for the losers. They are intoxicated by this freedom and amazed by the materialism, but inside they are still starving for something else. These things alone are not enough.

"So I use practical approaches, like when I had Bell's palsy that prevented me from even closing my eyelids. I told them God is like our eyelids; we take him for granted like the simple act of having eyelids that are like windshield-wiper blades to lubricate the eyes so we can see. That got it across. And I don't ask for volunteers for projects, for people to raise their hands or sign up on a sheet. I use a visual means so they can see exactly what is needed and who is meeting that need."

CCUC offers opportunities for spiritual growth and evangelism in many different forms—and languages. At the

Gen-X small group

Mandarin-language Bible study held on Wednesday nights, Rev. Chao produces a weekly newsletter with relevant scriptural passages, inspirational bonbons and the names and e-mail addresses of new people who attended the previous Sunday. On the Wednesday I attend, the four women and seven men pray for their own spiritual needs and the sick among them (one facing surgery for a brain tumor, another having horrible dreams with Satan all too present), but then pray for a missionary in Romania who works in the market-place where ethnic Chinese congregate and is attempting to establish a Christian fellowship. The universal church is present in this simple room that is used for language classes during the day and will see many other different uses before this group will meet there again.

In Amy Li's living room on Friday evening, a group of twenty-something ABCs in stocking feet—their shoes at the door, showing proper Chinese respect for the hostess—play a game of Balderdash to break the ice before tackling John 6:25–40. Key Wong is among them, but it is Todd Huynh, a sturdily built printing salesman who presides from his Barcalounger. This is the Chinese Generation X, and their occupations—pharmacy college student, teacher, computer programmer, web site developer, investment broker—are as varied as any gathering randomly chosen from among this age and economic group. They are well educated, they wear the right clothes, and they are or will soon be earning substantial salaries. They know well the seduction of the secular American way of life.

But as they ponder Todd's well-thought-out questions ("What is the real bread of life? How do we partake of *this* bread of life?") it is obvious they are trying to put the tires of religious belief to the road of their own lives. Todd tells of the temptation to go for the sale, regardless of who has to be

✦ 3. LAY INVOLVEMENT: MATCHING NEEDS WITH FACES ✦

Rev. Tsang has an ingenious way to encourage and to dramatize lay involvement. Periodically, he draws a chart of congregational needs and outreach. At each place where a person is required, there is a small, empty nail. Next to it, he places small pictures of each member of the congregation, with a tiny hole at the top of the picture. The challenge is obvious. Here you are. There are the tasks that need to be done. Who will do what?

stepped on, and splitting the commission with greedy purchasing agents. In pharmacy school, when others are cheating, what is she to do? A teacher tells of losing vision of what she was doing, of just seeing papers, not children.

And over in the church basement, David Lin is sketching out who believes and why on a transparency projected on a screen. Before him is the Ambassadors Club, college students from the University of Chicago, state universities, and many good private colleges. With a flurry of articles from *U.S. News &World Report* and *Time,* excerpts from a book and the *Chicago Sun-Times,* he presents modern research about the Bible's origins and authenticity of the Dead Sea Scrolls—and therefore the scripture that forms the basis of Christian belief.

But, interestingly, no scripture is quoted to make points; this fast-talking, energetic young man in T-shirt, jeans, and an open sweater vest utters no pious religious phrases. His is a logical treatise that the scripture in use today can be relied upon.

These are just two of six "clubs" that meet each Friday evening for religious training and spiritual growth—each program tailored to that age group, from third grade on up. On Saturday evenings once a month married couples of the Josiah Fellowship and their children gather together for— no, not a covered-dish dinner, but rather excellent Chinese food from a neighborhood restaurant (the idea is to make it not a chore, but a break to come). But even here, the groups are carefully divided between those with young children and those with older children, and both the speakers and the scriptural reflections help parents see their jobs within a Christian framework.

CCUC's multifaceted approach has produced a rich bounty of practicing Chinese Christians, not merely Chinese Christians in name or on the rolls of a church they rarely attend. CCUC is their extended family, their home. They may live a block away in a crowded Chinatown apartment or in a four-bedroom home in Chicago's wealthiest suburbs, but this church remains the focus of their lives and faith.

People like . . .

. . . Zunde Weng, a brilliant thirty-nine-year-old biologist who suffered through the Cultural Revolution and finally made his way to England and then the United States. "The biggest event of my life was the Tiananmen Square massacre. I had nothing to do with religion before then, but I opened the Bible and there were the words: If a son asks for bread his father will not give him a stone. The students asked for free-dom of thought and they were given bullets. That was the government in which I had put so much trust. But it was this church that, shall we say, made this real for me. My wife was lonely here, I was lonely, my two-year-old was lonely, and this church took us in. But I fought it for six years, because I could not really believe there was a God. I believed in biol-ogy. Finally, I saw there were both."

. . . or a plant manager, who must remain anonymous, who

the Chinese government sent to America to get his M.B.A. After paging through book after book in the Pui Tak bookstore, he began thinking. When he found he could do nothing but become a Christian, he was baptized in a church outside Chinatown. He knew he would have to return to China, and while his newfound faith would have to be kept a secret there, he vowed to begin a Christian underground in his factory to spread this good news he had learned about in Chicago.

. . . or Kin Lau, who came from Hong Kong in the 1970s and worked long hours in Chinese restaurants while pursuing an engineering degree. "Taller than the average Chinese," he jokes about his lean five-foot-eleven-inch frame. He found an outlet for his volleyball prowess in the CCUC gym, as well as a welcoming community. "At school, there were mostly Caucasians, not too eager to be friends. And even with the welcome I received here, I sniffed at Christianity. Chinese culture is five thousand years old, the Great Wall, three thousand. This was only two thousand years old. But I began to see that while Confucianism taught a way to act, Christianity was about a transformation from the inside out. It was a battle of cultures. Cheat on taxes? Cheat on a test? Work hard, give everything for the job like a good, loyal Chinese? I began to see that if I pleased my boss by taking on more and more work, but ruined my family, didn't spend time with my wife, what did it all mean? The old Chinese way was that work was the priority, that the father was the authority figure, period. I learned another way through this church, a balance in life, a real relationship with my children."

. . . or Jessica Jue, who looks up from her plate of dry-fried string beans and Kung Pao chicken at the Saturday night couples get-together to explain what this church means to her. She pats her husband, Wing, on the hand, and says, "After all, marriage was designed by God. When I come here, when I read scripture, when I pray, all I am doing is going back to the designer for instructions. To be honest, sometimes the zealousness of some Christians turns me off. I don't find that here."

. . . or Mike Set, who was featured in a new version of the New Testament called "My City, My God," which is geared to teenagers. "Because I'm the oldest son in the family, my parents expected me to do great things. Their dream for me was to have a decent bank account, big home, marry the right girl, have good kids, and drive a nice car—the American dream." After earning admission to Chicago's top high school, life fell apart for Mike, who even contemplated suicide. Although he considered church something for the weak, a friend convinced him to try CCUC's Young Teen Fellowship. "I sensed they had something I didn't have. There was a joy in their lives that I wanted for my life, too." He joined and began to experience something he had never felt before—that fulfillment, that joy he had seen in other teens.

Theirs is a gentle brand of evangelical Christianity at CCUC, firmly held—and sometimes chosen at a cost—but one wonderfully tempered by a long Chinese history of both learning and spirituality. For instance, Zunde, although an ardent Christian, is still a first rate biologist, and he is not about to blindly throw out evolution to accept a creationist view of the world.

These Christian threads spun at CCUC are woven throughout the complex tapestry that is Chinese-American life in Chicago. And as the music wafts out over Wentworth Avenue, coming from the CCUC speakers, it is just another reminder of a calm, sure—and thinking—Christian presence in the secular marketplace. The music is soft and appealing, but the message is a strong, unflinching one. CCUC is a church that is ever aware of its potential audience and does everything it can to reach them.

8

Full Gospel Church of God in Christ

1031 North Claiborne Avenue
New Orleans, LA 70116
504-821-6289
www.fullgospelcogic.com

✦ POINTS OF EXCELLENCE ✦

1. 6-point program—Ministry to the whole person

2. Undershepherd Nurturing Ministry

3. Boys II Men program

When Charles Brown first stood before the building on North Claiborne Avenue in New Orleans, he felt a compelling urge to walk in, to tell the owner that he wanted to start a church and—for some reason he couldn't even explain to himself—he wanted to start it *here*. Charles knew well the checkered history of the place—at one time the Claiborne Theatre was a whites-only movie house and, years later, a place where African Americans like himself were condescendingly assigned to the balcony. In its newest incarnation, the Claiborne was a disco, a popular gathering spot of not the greatest repute.

Today, as he stands before what has become the Full Gospel Church of God in Christ, the roar of traffic on Interstate 10, elevated on this stretch through the heart of New Orleans, is so much music to his ears. It is neither one of New Orleans's prettiest neighborhoods, nor the safest—hardly a promised land. It is still a neighborhood more known for the drug dealers and prostitutes who offer their various answers to coping with a poverty of means or a poverty of spirit. But to Charles Brown, Full Gospel is nothing less than a "beautiful oasis in the middle of the inner city," a place that stands as both a symbol and a reality that God has not moved to the suburbs, that transformation is always possible, that there is hope where none might readily be seen.

The Reverend Dr. Brown, the forty-eight-year-old pastor of Full Gospel, sees his work as not only saving souls but also changing lives. And what he has accomplished in the twenty-three years since he walked into Claiborne Theatre and confronted a somewhat shocked manager with his dream is testimony to a grand vision, perceptive insight—and plenty of hard work.

"It does no good to 'save' a person who has no job, no education, no hope," he says as we walk through his front doors and toward his tiny office just off the vestibule. "My work is with the total person, their soul and their body. Too many times Pentecostal, evangelical churches have worked on the emotions, the whooping and hollering, 'oh, the Spirit is upon

Pastor Charles Brown, Sunday morning

us' kind of thing. Altar calls, not enough." He shakes his head. "Not enough."

Pastor Brown over the years, in an inventive mixture of solid biblical, psychological, and cultural principles, has crafted what he calls ministry to the whole person, six touchstones for a healthy, holy life. "I try to teach that being successful in all six areas is what makes up a complete person. Because without any of these six, something is lacking and that person will constantly feel lacking, wanting.

"Too many churches never address the practical," he continues. "For example, while kids learn about sex, they learn it on the street. What single mothers face—the church never addresses these things, they shy away from them, embarrassed. We are dealing with a broken people who have been led to believe that they are worthless. People come through these doors depressed, despondent, hopeless, miserable. But if you teach them these simple principles, they can see how worthy and good they are and how practical—and possible —a life with God can be. An abundant life."

And the stories researcher Marty Minchin and I heard on our visits to Full Gospel were not just about people growing

> ### ✦ 1. 6-POINT PROGRAM — MINISTRY TO THE WHOLE PERSON ✦
>
> "Man is *spiritual*," Pastor Charles Brown begins a summary of a Full Gospel program that has transformed drug addicts, ex-convicts, and welfare mothers into productive citizens and zealous church members. "Man needs the Bible to instruct him, church participation to challenge him. *Mental*—education and the use of a person's mind are central. *Physical*—we honor the body. *Emotional*—love and hate, happiness, sadness are all part of the human condition, and we must understand them all. *Financial*—hard work, budgeting, saving are crucial. And *relational*—no man is an island; and going to church but not loving one's family is to miss this crucial point of human wholeness."

spiritually. People had gotten educations and decent-paying jobs, bought houses, gotten off welfare, stopped sleeping around, and conquered drug habits. Too many churches they had previously attended, Full Gospel members told us, only taught how to get to heaven and didn't bother to tell people how to live their lives in the here and now.

The programs at Full Gospel are impressive. Just outside Pastor Brown's office, a summer children's program for some one hundred children is under way. Unfettered by limited space, the children are broken into groups and sprinkled throughout the sanctuary. And these are neighborhood kids, not necessarily congregants' kids, as many Full Gospel members live outside the area. "Its purpose is basically twofold," Gloria Brown, the director, explains later. "We want them to have something to do during the summer, but we want to keep them on track when they go back to school." That involves everything from exercises in character-building to conflict resolution, leadership, and sometimes what Gloria calls "pre-dating." "Some of them think they're ready to date, and you have to tell them they're not, in a nice way," she says.

A college program aggressively seeks out African American students who will be attending New Orleans schools and provides them with not only a church home but a home away from home when—in the Adopt a Student program at Full Gospel—they are invited to parishioners' homes. Word of mouth in local colleges spreads the word that this is a good and welcoming church.

An innovative lay ministry program, the Undershepherd Nurturing Ministry, provides a "minipastor" for every ten to twenty families. A food and coat drive has developed into a door-to-door evangelization effort that has gotten behind doors that hid both material and spiritual poverty to reveal people hungry for a way to change their lives. Led by Lewis Davis, the Full Gospel evangelization team put on a block party at a nearby housing project—with free food, games for the children, and a gospel message. "We want to draw these people in because the Lord has put it in our spirit that we have people dying all around us, not physically, but spiritually," says Evelyn Croff, another evangelization leader. "We're here right in the middle of it, a great opportunity."

Full Gospel is a member of perhaps the fastest-growing Protestant denomination in the United States, the Church of God in Christ. COGIC is a predominantly African American church, whose roots are in both American slavery and a new wave of religious fervor that coalesced in the later part of the nineteenth and early part of the twentieth centuries. The

✦ 2. Undershepherd Nurturing Ministry ✦

Over a ten-week period, Pastor Charles Brown trains lay members of his congregation to be pastors to a group of ten to twenty families, which becomes, in essence, their minicongregation. The key word is *nurturing*. These lay people celebrate births, new jobs, graduations with their families. They are there in time of need, in sickness or death. "When you see Brother Bob," says Charles Brown, "I want people to realize they are seeing me, they are seeing Full Gospel. No pastor can tend to people at this intense level, but when you have so many people throughout the community, they can be my eyes and ears—and the heart of the church." Monthly meetings and short forms keep the undershepherds focused on their work and provide a continuing stream of information for Pastor Brown. "In Pentecostal churches, we have a phrase: 'Close the back door.' This means that people might join a church, but then they tend to wander out the back door if they aren't tended to. The undershepherds close that back door."

church is commonly known as Holiness or Pentecostal because of its focus on the events of Pentecost, when the power of the Holy Spirit descended upon the disciples, transforming them into fearless preachers of a revolutionary way of approaching God.

But, as we sit talking in his office, Charles Brown hardly looks like a revolutionary or a fiery activist. He is a man of ample girth, with a pleasant, round face; that uncle of yours who might work as an accountant for a public utility or own a dry cleaning business. He is surrounded by bald eagles—statues, photos, paintings, clock, calendar. It is his favorite and signature image—soaring, perhaps a representation of his own determination. This is a man who sees his work as nothing short of transforming a culture riddled with poverty, poor education, and low—or no—expectations into the possible, powerful kingdom of God.

Jarrod Short, with his shaved head and easy, streetwise mannerisms, is at twenty-three exactly the kind of young man that Charles Brown has in his sights. "Look, the way I was raised as a kid was, 'Now don't you go bringing me home some grandkids,'" Jarrod says as the summer program children stream to their next activity, some of them reaching out to grab his hand. "There was nothing about gifts, about what a person might be able to do; it was all about staying out of trouble." Jarrod received a Catholic education, but "it was the kind where you were a Christian on Sunday morning and the rest of the week was up to you. When I came in to Full Gospel and heard Pastor Brown, this was something different. This was a Christianity you could wear all week long."

Throughout his ministry, Pastor Brown has put great emphasis on men—young men and boys—because he believes they are the most endangered African Americans, who too often feel the street is their only platform and its rules their own justification. His Boys II Men program has made a strong statement that there are other ways to approach life.

"The call of the church has to be as strong as the call of the street," Charles says. "On the street, young men learn about false love, the love you get when you're on top, when you can get over, when you have a flashy car or ring or girlfriend. We teach them about God's love, a love that stays with them through good times and bad, a love that never abandons them, a love they don't have to prove anything to receive."

✦ 3. Boys II Men program ✦

Every Tuesday evening, Pastor Charles Brown gathers young men—with some older role models also there, men who have navigated these same mean streets but have found Jesus to be the best companion they could have—to talk both topically and biblically. For instance his "No Place Like Home" evening acknowledged that kids do want to leave home, that they feel their parents are too tough on them, and that once out of their homes life will be blissful and free. Then he counters with the story of the Prodigal Son and shows that the "world" is not as wonderful as they might think and that, for the time being, the best place to be is exactly where they are.

And while he is working on men, his wife, Connie Brown —the congregation refers to her as "Lady Connie"—oversees the women's ministry. It is an interesting marriage and partnership. She is the pastor's second wife, a Full Gospel member "nominated" by the congregation to be Pastor Brown's new spouse after his first wife died nine years ago. She is both deferential to her husband as pastor and the scripturally appointed head of the family and a powerful woman in her own right, determined to carry out her part of the ministry of this church. Her husky voice exudes an Oprah Winfrey-like confidence; she runs a nearby day care center, preaches in her husband's absence, and oversees many of the church's ministries.

On a Saturday morning when her highly organized Women's Fellowship Ministry meets, the theme being "cleanliness," it is quickly apparent that her husband's holistic approach is also her own. First, the group addresses physical cleanliness, covering topics from the negative side effects of carbonated drinks to how rubbing potatoes under the arm will prevent deodorant from irritating the skin to keeping their homes clean. The atmosphere in the sanctuary (if any church has a multipurpose room, it is Full Gospel's sanctuary) is hardly stiff or preachy. It is a gathering of women sharing their household secrets (don't put too much detergent in the washing machine because it will dull colored towels) and laughing about the intimacies of life (the toilet bowl and the poor aim of too many men).

They move on to spiritual cleanliness, which leads to an equally candid discussion of fasting as a way to keep the spirit clean. And again, the leader doesn't offer biblical mandates without translation into practical application. They talk about whether they should have sex when they fast, look up a scripture passage that states that women should ask their husbands' permission to fast, and debate whether it is OK to use fasting as a way to lose weight.

"If you don't grow at Full Gospel, it's only because you don't want to," says Janice Orajiato, forty-one, a charter member of Full Gospel. "We don't just talk about the Bible. We talk about everyday things they can use when they leave the church." Janice is one of those who finally decided to take Charles Brown at his word that God would provide if the people followed the biblical mandate to be generous to Him.

Even though she was having trouble paying her bills, Janice began to take out 10 percent of each paycheck to give to the church, and then worked with the remainder. "Then, it was like my money, it stretched, it went a little farther," she says. If she was short $40, someone in church would unknowingly give her that exact amount, saying that the Lord told them Janice needed a little extra help that month. Other times, when she paid her bills, the company would tell her that she had been overcharged. "I found out this stuff really works if you do it the way the Bible says. I'm just so blessed from being here. It just changes your whole outlook, your whole attitude."

"Our church is all about relationships," says Connie Brown. "We try to impress upon people that this is your new family. You can depend on us. You are going to be treated with love and respect here in ways you might never have been treated before. That's why we named our children's group the Kingdom Kids, because every one of them will be treated like royalty."

With an architect's rendering of a $1.2 million expansion project proudly displayed in the vestibule, a project that would dramatically change the complexion of this block of North Claiborne Avenue, Pastor Brown is undertaking what he knows is a difficult task. "We have some people with Ph.D.'s who understand entrepreneurial ways, but we have more people making minimum wage and working blue-collar jobs who find it hard to pay the bills, much less find money to give to a building project that hasn't even broken ground yet. But this is a church that is not about scraping by, this is a church that believes in excellence in everything we do."

Some churches shy away from preaching about giving, while others are criticized for preaching that prosperity is the primary sign of God's blessings. But once while admiring the lavish hotels on a trip to Las Vegas, Pastor Brown said the spirit spoke to him, saying that this is what God meant when He said, "Build." "Everything God does is with quality," Pastor Brown says. He believes that having money is a necessary part of abundant living and ministry. It's wrong, he says, for young people to see that the only ones who are prosperous are the rappers and the drug dealers, especially in a city that African

Assistant Youth Minister Jarrod Short

Americans perceive as lacking in opportunities. He believes that God's ministries and churches should reflect financial excellence as well.

"You can't have excellence without financial support," he says. Members are openly asked to give at least $20 a week, and, before the collection, they are encouraged to hold their white offering envelopes in the air and wave them around while someone prays. At Tuesday night church school, where the congregation is divided into seven small groups, they run a weekly offering competition. At the end of the night, the groups that exceed their weekly offering goal—from the children's group to the senior adult Bible study—are celebrated with cheering and clapping.

"Even with a lot of people who do face terrific financial restraints, we have one of the highest-percentage tithing churches in the country; some 90 percent of our people tithe," Pastor Brown says proudly.

The hub for the many spokes of the Full Gospel wheel is its Sunday service, a spirit-filled, prayerful, joyful, three-hour experience, but—and Charles Brown is adamant on this point—also an intelligent and practical approach to life. On a sweltering July Sunday, it is another packed house as Pastor Brown embarks on the third sermon in his series "The Christian Crowns," this time talking about three ways that Christians, once saved by grace, can earn the crown of righteousness.

He carefully lays his first and second points—an admonition to fight to win the battle within ourselves between the spirit and the flesh and then to persevere—before his people, but when he reaches his third point, a noticeable stir rises up among the congregation. Pastor Brown's voice gets higher, his sermon lapsing into half speech, half song. His dark gray dress shirt now drenched with sweat from his neck halfway down his torso, the pastor roams off the stage and up and down the aisles. His voice grows louder, his sentences shorter; the congregation's "amen"s more frequent and urgent.

"Keep the faith!"

"Don't let anything shake your faith!"

"Stay in the word of God!"

His son, Chuck, plays chords on the keyboard that accompany the pitch of Pastor Brown's sermon, turning it into an impromptu praise tune. The crowd responds to the building spiritual crescendo, waving their hands in the air, calling out "Amen!" and "Hallelujah!" Church members sway to the music, clapping in time with Chuck's rhythm, leaning their heads back, eyes closed. Four elderly ladies in the front row ease out into the open area below the stage, turning to the right as if on cue, dancing in a line up the right aisle. Congregation members peel out of the rows of chairs to form a conga line that snakes through the sanctuary.

This is the "whoop," a long-standing tradition in African

American Pentecostal churches when sermon turns to song and spiritual ecstasy is given free reign. Sometimes criticized for emphasizing dramatics over actual teaching and for manipulating the congregation's emotions, the "whoop" evolved from the early Negro churches, where pastors had no access to education because of their color and had to draw on their own experiences, emotions, and love for the scripture to make their point.

But at Full Gospel, as with many progressive African American churches, Pastor Brown makes sure that his congregation has something to whoop about before the dancing starts. "He will not whoop until they've been given the whole body of the sermon," Connie remarks later. "A lot of pastors get real ministry mixed up with performance. It's not about making women cry. You can shout all you want to, but if it's all over when the music stops, we've sold our people short."

A recent visiting preacher made the mistake of beginning his sermon with a whoop, shouting out repeatedly that he had a word from God, but never quite saying what that was. He got blank stares back from the congregation. "We know when you're on it and when you're not," Connie says.

While he has a recognized Sunday morning pulpit, Charles Brown is not shy about where he might do his preaching, convincing, or arm-twisting on Monday morning as well. He is a regular visitor to New Orleans mayor Marc Morial's office, where he will talk about everything from changing the tax structure to police protection to housing code enforcement or sanitation services. He is not shy about putting résumés from his congregants on the mayor's desk, or turning out hundreds of his people for a demonstration. His church, along with eighty-six others in New Orleans (including St. Peter Claver, which is featured in *Excellent Catholic Parishes*), have banded together to form ACT—All

Congregations Together—which multiplies their power in their neighborhoods and in the city at large.

His belief in lifelong education and the need to develop strong leaders instigated the creation of the Greater New Orleans Fellowship School of Ministry. Here, lay leaders and ministers can take classes in all areas of biblically based leadership. "I saw a need for people to understand excellence in ministry," he says, "even down to simple ideas like getting tasks done on time. I was trained by Southern Baptists; I believe in organization," he adds, smiling his beatific smile.

Judy White, a forty-year-old quiet-natured mother of two sons, could be a poster child for Pastor Brown's emphasis on education within a holistic ministry. Judy had two sons out of wedlock and spent years bouncing back and forth between dead-end jobs and welfare. But when she began attending Full Gospel and listened to Pastor Brown's teachings for several years, she slowly began making changes in her life. She eventually enrolled in a welfare-to-work training program and is now employed at a day care center. "It was like regrouping, being reprogrammed," she says. "Sitting under his ministry has made all the difference to me."

The rest of her life changed as well. Pastor Brown's teaching showed her that having sex outside of marriage wasn't right—she's now been abstinent for seven years. She struggled with debt for years, and in 1999 her credit was cleared. And Pastor Brown and his Boys II Men program are helping her raise her boys with solid values.

"At one time, I was a very mean and hateful person," she admits. "Now it's like the love of God has really changed me. Now it's hard for some people to grasp that I was like that. Everything was like me, myself, and I, and now it's, 'What can I do for you?' Now, once I lay my head on my pillow at night, I know I did my best."

Gloria Brown first appears the picture of confidence. She is a tall, striking woman with long, curly hair, and a master's degree in education. "Oh, man," she answers when asked what she used to be like. "I was a person who suffered from low self-esteem. I guess I really didn't know who I was in Christ."

It was a simple act that began the change. After she attended Full Gospel for a year, Pastor Brown asked her to read the announcements during the Sunday service. She was "scared to death," but she got through the reading. This, however, was only the beginning. Charles Brown saw potential in Gloria that she didn't see in herself. Now, she regularly leads workshops for her peers, heads the church's citywide summer camp, coordinates Vacation Bible School, and recently graduated from the School of Ministry—and yes, she still reads announcements, loudly and clearly.

At the end of his day, his once-starched shirt now limp, Charles Brown and I walk along North Claiborne Avenue, past the shabby buildings, the known drug hangouts on his block. "It will take time, but we will transform lives, we will transform our block. If I can only keep my vision," he says, not for lack of confidence but more as a note on the refrigerator to remind him to do something.

"I cannot posture, I cannot say I know everything, that I make no mistakes. I cannot be arrogant. I am dealing with wounded people, so I need to be a wounded healer. It's not about the whoop. It's about a new style and doing some things that go against the style of a typical African American preacher. Being transparent to your people goes against it too, but that's what we have to do if we are to truly and deeply succeed. I have to be that wounded healer."

9

Warehouse 242

1213 West Morehead Street, Suite C
Charlotte, NC 28208
704-344-9242
www.warehouse242.org

+ POINTS OF EXCELLENCE +

1. Sharing life with non-Christians—maximizing points of contact

2. C.pak—a postmodern/biblical small community

3. Discerning gifts for ministry

On this Friday night in the Grady Cole Center, a civic auditorium in downtown Charlotte, North Carolina, the band is already up to speed: plenty of decibels, perfectly balanced acoustics, a throbbing beat. A great-looking crowd streams through the doors, by and large Gen Xers, dressed in shorts and tank tops, button-down shirts and Talbot's dresses—and many variations in between. Coffee urns, with a favorite syrup accent (amaretto? hazelnut?) await them in the lobby where they are given free designer travel mugs for their morning commute to work. When they arrive at their seats they find a coffee filter; yes, a coffee filter. I mean enough already. What's going on here?

To Todd Hahn, thirty-one, that pounding music blasting out from what looks, and sounds, like a rock band, is aural praise, the sound—to him—reminiscent of that within a soaring cathedral. And the coffee filters provide a perfect way to focus this, the Starbucks (actually it's Caribou coffee being served here in the South) generation, on what will be presented—and how it makes sense in their lives. "Each week, we work hard to have something people can take home with them. [He is not talking about the filters or the traveling mugs bearing his church's distinctive logo.] No white noise. My people just won't put up with it."

This is the weekly worship of Warehouse 242, one of America's cutting-edge-on-the-cutting-edge churches, and Todd this evening—although he won't actually be seen on stage until at least forty-five minutes into the service—will tell his congregation that they are grounds through which God pours his graces. They can provide that refreshing drink for the outstretched cups of a generation indeed thirsty for something beyond a latte. It is, admittedly, quite a variation on Paul's musings in First Corinthians, but Todd Hahn knows well how to connect with his generation.

Warehouse 242 grew out of a Sunday school class that Todd headed at Charlotte's Forest Hill Evangelical Presbyterian Church "that just seemed to take on a life of its own," he tells me earlier that afternoon. "People were exchanging phone numbers, talking before and after class, getting together out-

C. pak small group

side of class. It wasn't a church, but people thought of it as their church. Forest Hill was more for baby boomers, and they were younger and weren't completely at home there. It was obvious something was happening, the Spirit was leading us, we just had to follow." That Sunday school class eventually grew into a Saturday night service called satpm.com that quickly drew hundreds of Gen Xers. Todd, with the blessing and financial support of Forest Hill Church, then turned satpm.com into its own church.

Warehouse 242: A little strange as a name for a church, no? But as I page through the three-ring binder that contains the entire, but admittedly brief, history of a year-old church, its genesis is clear. After all, New Hope Community or Southend or Crossroads of Hope were simply not going to do as names for a Gen-X church for Charlotte's Center City, so at a marathon session with the best marketing minds this fledging congregation could muster, Warehouse 242 was thrown against the wall—and it stuck. Acts 2:42, where the first Christian churches were formed, is one part. "A warehouse is a temporary place where you hold things. Stuff comes in and out, stuff just doesn't sit there. Like churches should be, bringing people in, equipping them for life, and sending them back into the world," says Hahn. "It was perfect."

Warehouse 242 had actually been in the works, at least conceptually, since Todd was a college student at the University of North Carolina at Chapel Hill in the late-1980s. Jimmy Long, the leader of a Christian group on campus who later wrote a book about ministering to Generation X, told Todd that he would be part of a new generational ministry. "He said, 'There's something different about your generation,'" Todd said. "Something kind of went off in me when he said that."

As we sit in Todd Hahn's tiny office, a former bedroom within a rented house in Charlotte's South End that serves as the church's temporary administration building, this somewhat unconventional thirty-one-year-old pastor—with his penetrating blue eyes, red hair, earring, boundless nervous energy, jeans, and T-shirt—talks about the generation that churches are desperate to gather in, yet often find elusive.

"Everyone says Gen-X people are uncommitted; it's just that they need something real to be committed to," he begins. "These are children of divorce, many of whom have no church background; they are wary, mistrustful of institutions that have disappointed us all. They are a fragmented people adrift in an increasingly divided culture, skeptical of certainty and believing that life is terribly fragile and unpredictable. But, as disconnected as they feel, they are relational people. They long for deep relationships. They relate to individuals, to people, not to some idea or ideal or institutional line. They deal in realness rather than only what can seemingly be proved by intellect or reason. And they want to see continuity, where they fit in this confusing time. I saw, over and over again in that Sunday school class, that they wanted to give themselves to something beyond a sort of 'white bread' world that they live in, but they needed to see that that 'something' was tangible, that it would work. They process truth relationally, so if they see that a community like the one we hope we are building really does stand for something, will be there for them when things are going great and when they suck, then they'll commit to it.

"I feel very strongly, to the bottom of my being, that God has given us a mission here in Charlotte: to transform this city. And that he has chosen the local church to be the face of redemption, the means of redemption. These people are not antichurch. For many of them, the church isn't on the screen, not part of their equation. We really do think of ourselves as missionaries to North American culture."

Research shows that by 2003, Charlotte will be home to 317,000 Gen Xers, certainly a large and potentially influential part of the population. "And there is a real hunger in the postmodern culture to be rooted in something more than the contemporary," Hahn says. "They are much more deeply traditional than the baby-boomer generation, but traditional in different ways. If this city really does have more churches per block than any city in America—as some say—there would be no use in starting another one like those already here. If you want Sunday school, Sunday night church, and midweek worship, Warehouse 242 won't suit you. If you want a church that will go into every corner of your life, every day, here we are. People spend too much time in church; they need to take what church means into the world."

That church, Warehouse 242, is a strange combination of the very orthodox and the very contemporary. There are no fancy bulletins for the service, no standing committees (only ministries), the music is usually not Handel, and yet Todd

Hahn uses such Vatican II Catholic terms as "the priesthood of the believers," and he will process with a Celtic cross and sing a rock interpretation of the *Agnus Dei*. It is a church where phone calls are far rarer than e-mails, where non-Christians are called the "normal" people, and *lectio divina,* the ancient monastic practice of praying the scriptures, is encouraged.

As an Evangelical Presbyterian Church, Warehouse 242 is by doctrine and practice somewhat in between the Presbyterian Church (U.S.A.), the largest branch of Presbyterianism, which is considered theologically liberal, and the Presbyterian Church in America, which broke off in the early 1970s to maintain a more traditionalist approach. EPC requires all churches to hold to "essential" tenets of the Christian faith, but allows each congregation freedom in forming opinions on "nonessential" matters, such as whether women can be elected as deacons and elders. And, as one of the new models of churches fashioned entirely for postmodern generations, Warehouse 242 has distinctive differences. It does not have separate services for Christians and non-Christians, and it looks upon conversion as a continuing process, not something settled with an emotional altar call. "God brings people to him in different ways, at different paces," says Todd.

"Warehouse 242 has been a wild trip, but I wouldn't change it for anything in the world," says Chris Bradle, twenty-six, who has been on the dizzying ride for most of the year that Warehouse 242 has been in existence. "I never, ever, pictured church would be this good." His story, like that three-ring binder, provides a synopsis of the appeal of this postmodern church.

Chris had wandered in and out of Christianity his whole life. He moved to Charlotte from upstate New York after spending a weekend with relatives there and went to satpm.com to meet people. A church member talked him into joining a short mission trip to Nicaragua to build a medical clinic, even though he didn't feel spiritually qualified to go. He avoided interacting with the team before the trip, raising his funding without the help of team members and attending only two of the pre-trip meetings. "Work and other things kept me out of the meetings," he says. "I never really focused on the trip. My life was all out of order."

But the experience in Nicaragua changed him forever. He made friends he is still close to. And, even more significantly, his interest was peaked as the people on the trip talked about their ministry "teams." When they asked him what "team" he was on, he didn't have an answer.

"I had a really vague feeling when I left that I needed to get involved in something," he said. "Then it was a feeling of desperation. I called Todd and asked to be involved in the core group, and I was welcomed with open arms. At the first core group meeting I went to, I had no intentions of doing marketing—I do it all day long. But a lot of stuff happened real quickly."

To launch this new church, the core group of about ninety people talked of a twenty-thousand-piece mailing all over Charlotte, a typical move for starter churches. But Chris then studied Acts 2 and threw out all conventional advertising strategies. "We changed from mass mailing to personal invitation," he says. "It was surely from God, especially since I was in the mind-set of billboards and full-page ads."

Members of the core community were given business cards with a map to the community center where the first service would be held, the church address, phone number, and web site address and were instructed to invite their friends to the first Warehouse 242 meeting. Core community members had no idea how many would respond to this word-of-mouth advertising. Their only other means of "advertising"

✦ 1. SHARING LIFE WITH NON-CHRISTIANS — MAXIMIZING POINTS OF CONTACT ✦

Warehouse 242 funnels much of its energy into making sure that church members are always interacting with non-Christians, both in their spiritual lives and in their everyday lives. Members are encouraged to make close Christian friends but not to limit themselves there. Many church members purposely join "secular" organizations, such as an ultimate Frisbee league, to meet non-Christians whom they can eventually invite to church. They also make an effort to get to know non-Christians they are naturally in contact with at work or school and invite them to church—in fact, a recent survey found that 90 percent of the people who attend Warehouse who did not come from Forest Hill, Warehouse's mother church, came because a friend invited them.

Warehouse members also can commit to praying for non-Christians through "prayer triplets," an idea born in Warehouse's founding core group. Members were divided into groups of three, and each wrote down the names of three non-Christians they wanted to come to Warehouse 242. Each person in the group prayed for all nine people. "I've seen an amazing number of those people come here," says Jenny Lewis, Warehouse's office administrator.

was what they call "prayer triplets," where members committed to praying for non-Christians they knew.

To avoid unrealistic expectations, Todd told the core community to expect no more than 150 people, total, to attend the inaugural service. They were shocked when there was standing room only. Since then, attendance has been between 300 and 500 weekly, many of whom were on the prayer triplet cards. And, while many quickly growing churches like Warehouse 242 deal with growth by starting new ministries to handle the influx, here leaders have chosen to stick with their original intentions of doing three things well: small groups, the Sunday worship service, and community outreach.

Small groups, or C.pax, are the core of Warehouse's ministry. "Relationships are everything to postmodern people," says Stacy Pickerell, Warehouse's pastor of community, "but that makes complete sense in Christian context. God himself exists in community. As people who follow him, we too need to exist in community. It's not just reading the Bible together. It's about living life together."

That "living life together" approach is readily apparent at Warehouse, where the division between Christian and non-Christian that is often so obvious—and even encouraged—in traditional evangelical churches, is deemphasized. Instead of shying away from worldly culture, Warehouse leaders encourage members to live Christian lives *within* the culture. Behaviors that traditional churches frown upon, such as drinking and dancing, are not major issues here. In fact, on the staff biographies posted on the church's web site, several of the pastors list enjoying good beer and wine as a favorite activity.

Warehouse's goal is to funnel all members into a C.pak, but often newcomers to the Sunday service, especially non-Christians, are not immediately interested in joining a small group. These people are asked to do something, anything, even if it means standing at the door and saying hello to people coming in. The church also created "Hands on Warehouse," a group that meets an hour and a half before the

✦ 2. C.PAK — A POSTMODERN/BIBLICAL SMALL COMMUNITY ✦

C.pax (plural) are the "arteries and veins of Warehouse 242, people living together as conduits of service and grace throughout the community and serving real needs in Charlotte as a natural outflow of their life together," says Stacy Pickerell, pastor of community. Each C.pak (singular) is independent, each unique, each tailored to the needs of the participants, each open to interpersonal dynamics. "C" stands for community, and "pak" is a group of people moving through life together. All significant church announcements are made in C.pax, so if a person wants to be an active member of Warehouse 242, they must attend one of the more than twenty C.pax.

People relating to one another honestly in community, in action with the Bible, and in prayer are the three key elements. On alternate weeks, the groups discuss the previous week's sermon. They socialize together, do community service together, and in the process develop deep relationships. Real people talk about their lives and are "continually shocked by the love of God, expressed by his grace to us in Christ," says Stacy. And a love expressed by each other. These are real people, real lives, real community.

Sunday service to set up the chairs and sound equipment, as an easy way for people to get involved.

That was the way a twenty-something we'll call Ned found his way into Warehouse. Today he has a good job in sales, but before he found Warehouse 242, cocaine and crack were his sources of community and satisfaction. "I had run wild for long enough, was seeing so many lives go to hell, didn't want mine to go there, but couldn't figure a way out," he tells me as we stand outside the Grady Cole Center before the service. "This girl at work told me she'd visited this great place and I ought to try it. Funny, she stayed with her old church, but here I am. From the git-go, people were friendly, welcoming, none of this hand-you-a-program-and-give-you-a-smile stuff, they really wanted to know *me*. I never read the Bible before; now I'm working my way through John. I have friends; I help out here. This is the anchor for my life."

One of the most unusual aspects of Warehouse's C.pax is that they are designed for maximum interaction between Christians and non-Christians. While many Christians and churches use small groups as a place to retreat from the non-Christian world for prayer and Bible reading, Warehouse 242 is likely to disband a small group that doesn't have non-Christians—or "normal" people—attending. The purpose of the groups is not to build a Christian stronghold against the world, but to open discussions to non-Christians, who often provide new perspectives, and to build relationships between Christians and non-Christians, possibly the most effective method of evangelism.

Warehouse also discourages small groups made of similar people, such as an all-singles group or a group based on similar interests. "I think the more similar people in churches and small groups are, the more safe and hunkered down they become," Stacy says. "I think one of the strengths of C.pax is they're diverse. This keeps them on the edge."

The mission of a C.pak, then, is not only to "live life" with non-Christians but to grow and multiply, the result of more people, hopefully non-Christians, being brought into the C.pax communities. "Every C.pak should multiply within

Todd Hahn, Jenny Lewis, and Stacy Pickerell

six months," Stacy says, "and we won't let a C.pak just go on and on without accomplishing its mission. There's a definite sadness in multiplication because people get really close and it's terrible to break up, but look at the new people we're bringing in."

The stories of these "new" or "normal" people abound, often because non-Christians find that they are accepted at Warehouse regardless of spotty pasts or present hang-ups or habits. Many times, after weeks or months of observing the lives of people in a C.pak, the non-Christians begin asking questions of themselves. They find unexpected acceptance when they tell their life stories to the small group and find that the members still want to be their friends. "Postmoderns want to know what they're getting into," Stacy says. "There's an environment where honest questioning is really the norm and it is really OK."

One man, finally responding to two months of invitations from a Warehouse 242 member he worked with, hesitantly went bowling with her C.pak. The man was divorced, dealing with depression, and not much interested in the Christian faith. "He had anticipated 'bowling for Jesus,'" Stacy says. "But he got to smoke, and people were drinking beer. Two months later he gave his life to Christ."

The C.pak that researcher Marty Minchin attended met at a modest home in a marginal neighborhood in downtown Charlotte. Deb and Dennis Hopkins, an attractive, young, admittedly once-yuppie couple, had recently sold their suburban condo and moved to the primarily black neighborhood to put their beliefs on the line and to promote racial harmony. Several other Warehouse couples are contemplating moving to the same neighborhood.

The group that night was newly constituted, consisting of half the members of a recently divided C.pak. But that didn't hinder the frank discussion the members were obviously used to. They talked about the Sunday sermon, but the discussion strayed to everything from funny animal stories to the sex of Deb's baby to what to do when you want to invite your homosexual friends to church.

When it came time to pray, the requests were not just for someone's aunt's first cousin who was in the hospital or other impersonal requests. One woman, who knew only one other person in the group well, talked openly about breaking up with her boyfriend that weekend because he wouldn't commit to a serious relationship. Other people in the group followed up with questions, asking her about the situation. Deb and Dennis talked about getting used to hearing gunshots in their neighborhood, and they asked for people to continue praying for their new life there.

Mike Greene, the leader of this C.pak, who is married and has two children, said he and his wife, Kathy, had often attended small groups at other churches, but the meetings usually involved one person giving what amounted to a mini-sermon on his or her interpretation of that week's Bible verses. The Greenes felt little connection with the church or the other people in the small group, found the Bible study to be a yawner, and only went because they felt obligated. But their small group at Warehouse, they said, is life-giving, a place where they are growing spiritually.

Warehouse 242 uses the family atmosphere promoted in C.pax to counteract the sense of rootlessness that is so prevalent in young adults, many who have moved away from home to find jobs. Many Warehouse members don't live near family, and often they arrive in Charlotte not knowing anyone.

Jennifer Hibbard, twenty-six, graduated from Davidson College in 1998 and moved to Charlotte with her college roommate, hoping to get a job in social work. Instead, she found the satpm.com service and, on a whim, called Todd about a job opening he had for a ministry assistant. "I told him what he was describing was nothing like I'd ever planned on pursuing," she said. "Todd asked for a two-year commitment, which was not in my plan at all."

But Jennifer took the job, and she has also enrolled in a part-time program at the University of North Carolina at Chapel Hill to earn a master's degree in social work. Her two-year commitment with Warehouse is up, but she states emphatically that she is not moving anywhere. "I have roots here because of Warehouse."

Jennifer is by far not the only Warehouse member who has made major life decisions because of her involvement in the church and its community. One of the tenets of postmodern theology is that postmodern people sense that the world is random. To counteract that, pastors teach in terms of stories, that the gospel is a narrative that connects all of history together, and that people's lives have a place in that story. "There's such a longing for sense of place," Todd said. "We want them to see themselves as something bigger than they feel."

Postmodern preachers have also found that the sermons that worked with baby boomers—talks that address people's "felt needs" and have titles such as "How to Have a Healthy

Marriage" and "Handling Anger"—are not what postmoderns want to hear. "Older generations wanted content and Bible knowledge, preferring to be left to themselves to apply the teachings of the Bible to their lives: "*Is it true?*," Todd wrote in *GenXers After God,* which he coauthored with the psychologist David Verhagen. "Boomers demanded practical application: *Does it work for me?* Generation Xers are asking a fundamentally different question: *Does it matter?*"

In a recent sermon series on idols, Todd taught his congregation what idols were, focusing on sex, work, and appearance, major concerns of Charlotte's postmoderns; how to get rid of them; and what to replace them with. "Idols mess up and distort our thinking," he told his congregation. "They distort our emotions. We long for things more than we should." He taught about finding delight in God rather than in the things of the world. The sermons led to many out-of-church discussions, as members struggled to figure out what their own idols were. "It was pretty intense," said Chris Bradle. "It shook up everyone in the church. People were making changes in their lives once they found out what their idols were."

Such change is not an unusual outcome of Sunday's preaching or of life in the Warehouse community. When some members are faced with decisions such as what job to take or whether to move, they consider more than just the salary. Warehouse has taught people to rearrange their priorities and decide what is truly important. After the idols sermon series, and much thought and prayer, Chris Bradle quit his job as a senior graphic designer in a prestigious advertising agency.

"My job was too consuming," he says. "Everyone knew of me because of my job. It was doing a pretty bad job on me emotionally—I knew I needed to quit." He took over as head of Warehouse's marketing team, even though common sense might seem to direct him otherwise—trading a great job for unemployment and uncertainty. What Chris got in return—time to spend on what he has made a higher priority: to present the Warehouse 242 ideal to Charlotte—he considers a better choice. And he brings a professional excellence to his job.

Excellence at Warehouse 242 is not a result of some pie in the sky, naïve faith. Yes, the Warehouse 242 people feel God is working with and through them, but they are doing their part too. The church has a small ministry staff of seven, and the rest of the church's work, which is consistently outstanding, is done by volunteer ministry teams. The church's publicity and web site, for example, which Chris's marketing team handles, is slick and professional-looking. The worship team could hold its own with any.

This excellence is not left to the randomness of volunteerism; leadership at Warehouse is serious business. "We want to build a leadership culture," Todd says, "to be the best-led church in North America because if you're well led, then that results in the accomplishment of vision and ministry. It's about discerning what the vision is and how to accomplish it."

The pastoral team looks at where their members' ministry gifts lie, then approaches people with the job. "I think a lot of times people are doubtful of their abilities, but that's where we play such a huge role in it," says Stacy Pickerell. People are often shocked when they are asked to lead some Warehouse 242 effort, "many times because no one has ever told them that God has given them gifts that can be used for ministry."

Jenny Lewis, twenty-five, moved to Charlotte to take a mortgage banking job, and she was soon managing a large group of processors and was making enough money to buy a house. Stacey Pickerell asked Jenny to coffee one day—what Jenny thought was just a friendly visit—and presented

✦ 3. Discerning gifts for ministry ✦

Warehouse 242 emphasizes involvement—living out the Christian faith, they believe, requires applying one's gifts to ministry, be that setting up chairs before the Sunday service or leading a prayer group. To discern each person's gifts, he or she fills out a short (taking up only a quarter of a page) form, "Uniquely You," which asks what the person feels are his or her spiritual gifts (mercy, wisdom, serving, etc.), asks his or her personality type (characterized by D, I, S, or C—"Dominance," "Influence," "Steadiness," or "Compliance") and a "behavioral blend," each person's unique combination of the personality types.

When the results of the form are tabulated, the information provides at least a starting point for where the person can be best utilized. For example, someone determined to have the spiritual gifts of pastor/shepherd, wisdom, and teaching might be a good group leader. People who thrive in outreach and service will have the spiritual gifts of evangelism, serving and helps, exhortation, mercy, and faith.

Other ministry areas matched with spiritual gifts include finance and administration (giving, wisdom, faith); children's ministry (giving, serving/helps, mercy, wisdom); marketing and communications (evangelism, wisdom, faith); prayer (faith, knowledge, prophecy, wisdom); special forces/operations (serving/helps); guest services and assimilation (serving/helps, evangelism, exhortation); and worship (pastor/shepherd, serving/helps).

her with a seemingly preposterous job proposition. The Warehouse staff saw that Jenny had great administrative talents, and they wanted her as their office assistant, meaning less pay, less prestige, and maybe, no house.

"But I couldn't stop thinking about it," Jenny said. "I really struggled with what that change was going to mean for me." She took the job, and even though she's had trouble finding a third roommate to help with the mortgage on the new house, she's certain that she made the right choice.

New leaders are virtually born weekly at Warehouse 242, and members are involved in service projects ranging from work with unwed mothers to men at a city shelter, disabled kids, and flood relief. An impressive start, to be sure. The lives of hundreds of Gen Xers are filled with the excitement and the demands of a church they never anticipated finding —or joining.

And in the Grady Cole Center, the service for this Friday evening has ended. The burlap backdrop, the stark metal pipe (Warehouse's "Metallica Cross") that is the stage's focal point, and the screen that projected PowerPoint scriptural quotations and highlights from Todd Hahn's talk will soon come down. Warehouse 242 people are not eager to leave; these are their friends—or new acquaintances to make, in a place that speaks a different language about their worth, their place, their potential. A place unlike the bar or health club where they might seek companionship, a place where their deepest selves are the issue, not what the world sees on their surfaces.

The coffee filters for the most part remain on the seats; not too many are taken home. But certainly in the week ahead, when those who were here tonight see a coffee filter in a favorite coffee shop or in their kitchen or at work, they might just be reminded. What are those graces of God pouring through in their lives? What drink are they offering to the world?

Final Thoughts

I have been both blessed—and distressed—by this journey through some of the best Protestant congregations in America. At each stop, I have seen the Spirit of God alive in the world, in people's lives. I have seen people happy to be good, to be decent, to be making a difference in the world, and willing to change. These are people who sense that God is not far away or beyond their reach or deaf to their needs, but right there in the midst of their untidy, imperfect lives, just as he has promised to be.

I have been distressed because once being in these wonderful homes for the spirit, what was happening in them looked so possible and accessible I wanted this experience for everyone who turns to a church for succor or guidance. The churches in this book, along with George Bernard Shaw—though not especially considered a man of conventional belief—point so clearly to what a life of faith can mean: "You see things; and you say, 'Why?' But I dream things that never were; and I say, 'Why not?'"

Something quite amazing is happening in our day. A culture of religious practice is collapsing. In the Catholic tradition that collapse has seen a diminution of the obligation that propelled many a Catholic to church on Sunday. In the Protestant world, denominational affiliation apparently does not have the irresistible pull it once did, ensuring generation would follow generation into a specific sect, or even type, of church.

As Kortright Davis observes, "There often comes a time in the life of the church when codes and customs, values and virtues, even words and symbols, become worn and jaded. They seem to lose much of their force and efficacy and no longer command any authority in people's lives."[1]

But to bemoan the mixture of institutional chaos and individual confusion that has accompanied this collapse is to miss the point: People are focusing less on church and more on God. The culture of religion in post–World War II America—a thin and remarkably fragile patina of institutionalized belief so vividly portrayed by Will Herberg in *Protestant–Catholic–Jew: An Essay in American Religious Sociology*—has in many ways been dissolved. People realize that window dressing is not enough—for no one is looking in the window anymore. People want to see and experience what's in the store, not simply be its lifeless mannequins. In place of that static window dressing on display each week is the possibility of a loving presence not only for that Sunday hour, but throughout the week.

And so this sea change in our religious culture may not be such a bad thing, if it can be seen for what it is. Denominations had their foundations in social class, ethnicity, race,

[1] Kortright Davis, *Serving with Power: Reviving the Spirit of Christian Ministry* (Mahwah, NJ: Paulist Press, 1999).

and region perhaps more than their differences in dogma or doctrine. In our mobile nation public education, intermarriage, and media saturation have pierced once impervious social—and religious—membranes. We are an unfettered, unconfined people. But we are still individuals whose souls long for a lasting relationship that will be with us through the various seasons of our journey through life. Our souls are restless until they are connected to that great power that is God.

But, paradoxically, while denominational affiliation might appear to be less and less relevant, it is actually very important. A recent survey shows that a significant number of people still see themselves as the standard bearers of their various traditions. But there is a crucial difference today.

What the Parish/Congregation Study found in this national search for excellent churches is that respondents are apparently not referring per se to Lutheranism or Methodism or to evangelical Protestantism. Their enthusiasm, affiliation, and affection come from the fact that they have found *a* church that has stirred their souls, and *that* church happens to be of a certain kind. It was *that* church that gave them both something to reach for and something to hang on to. It is apparent that the local church is crucially important—far more important than broad institutional posturing—as the local church is still the locus for belief, the point of entry for the seeker, the school for learning a new way to live, and the launching pad into the world.

That local church—a specific, identifiable island amid the storm that is all our lives—is what attracts them, a church with enough compassion and imagination, which commands —and, they would say, deserves—a certain authority over their lives. For it is a new kind of authority, not belligerent or righteous or doctrinal, but rather an authority that wells up from that pure spring that is the life and word of Jesus Christ. It is a practical, proved, deserved authority, not one that demands obeisance but rather because, simply put, it is an authority that makes sense and is ultimately good for them.

As I was not able to name the ideal or best Catholic parish, I am doubly stumped as I look across the Protestant landscape. It is far too varied, too rich, too fluid to attempt such an assessment. What I have done is list some of the common traits I found in these excellent churches in the next section. But if I were to single out a trait that seems to sum up their excellence it would be something I would call—and I know this is a strange combination of words—a "missionary authenticity."

These excellent churches look about them as if for the first time, put aside assumptions, and try to understand who indeed these people are and how they might be served. And they do it with an authenticity that is immediately apparent and enormously attractive. Now that I think about it, isn't authenticity just another word for the "habit of being" I spoke of in the introduction? Somehow, some way, these churches have broken through the sclerotic buildup of dead practices and policies that no longer work and have opened up free-flowing channels of grace. They have suffered through changes and new beginnings while often being chastened or even condemned by voices of doom around them. Blessed are these risk-takers for they have once again revealed the kingdom of God.

I have certainly not found all the excellent churches in America, just some of them. I'm sure there are many more. But what the Parish/Congregation Study shows—and the churches profiled in this book confirm—is that excellence has nothing to do with size, location, resources, denomination or lack of one. Just a quick look at the magnificent variety and impact of these nine churches is proof enough: in rural Lone Wolf, Oklahoma, transforming an area God seemed to have forgotten; in Worcester, Massachusetts, sanctifying mean streets; in Denver, bringing God to where people live; in Washington, D.C., changing an entire neighborhood; in Charlotte, drawing young adults to serve their community and each other; in New Orleans, providing an oasis in the midst of destitution; in Santa Monica, shaping a new way of living; in Birmingham, providing answers to questions that gnaw at the heart; in Chicago, welcoming new immigrants while prodding the American-born to new heights.

They are beacons to us all, signs that if we trust in God, God will be with us. A living, daily God. This is not window dressing.

Common Traits of
Excellent
Congregations

These traits are the distillation of the qualities found in the churches written about in this book. Excellent churches might not have all of these traits, but they will have many of them. I offer them as a sort of template for what constitutes an excellent church, at least as determined by those of us involved in the Parish/Congregation Study. I have gathered them under the categories of approach, the work, community, spirituality, and structure.

APPROACH

1. *A vibrancy, an excitement about living a Christian life*

By this I don't mean some sort of generic happiness, the "have a good day" school of life. It is far deeper than that, and sometimes far more painful than one might imagine. Excellent churches live on "the edge," the creative and holy edge that the New Testament both stipulates and forecasts. Being a Christian is not a leisure-time activity but a high-adventure pursuit. These churches have accepted this challenge, and it brings an excitement to what they do. For each day, each activity, each gathering, each meeting is brimming with possibilities, and these churches want to seize those possibilities. They revel in the challenge. Yet, along with this excitement is a quiet peace, a trust that God walks with them.

2. Entrepreneurial

These are risk-takers; self-starters, they use what works in pastoral practices and they put aside that which does not. They live George Bernard Shaw's words, "and dream things that never were." Excellent churches are constantly looking for better ways to reach and serve people. This entrepreneurial spirit is not about accumulating a particular number of conversions but about genuinely doing a better job so that people naturally not only want to come to this church, but also want to be a part of it.

3. Draw not geographically or even denominationally, but philosophically

Notice, I did not say "religiously." The approach, the style of these churches, attracts people beyond their normal neighborhood or area and often draws people from outside their denomination (or nondenomination). The vision of excellent churches transcends such artificial boundaries. People are drawn to them because they sense that the spirit of a living God is present—a spirit that will not be encumbered by names, titles, or traditions, or lack of them.

4) *Reach beyond their comfort zone*

Whether this means reaching beyond what might be considered their usual constituency or their usual practices, excellent church members are not afraid of being uncomfortable. They ask the tough questions about themselves. (Who are we? What sort of image are we presenting to the world? What would Jesus do in this situation? Are we doing enough?) They are not afraid to walk into city hall, or over to the next desk in their office, or to reach across the back fence if they know that is where they need to be. In essence, they have denied themselves a comfort zone for now so that they see themselves as a new (while certainly imperfect) creation; those old taboos are gone, polite convention no longer rules. While they are not belligerent or righteous, they have a new power to go places they would never have dreamed of going, to let words come from their mouths they might once have kept secret in their hearts.

5) *Regularly evaluate themselves*

In terms of pastoral and sacramental effectiveness, excellent churches have unconsciously adopted a certain kind of "zero-based budgeting" approach where convention or convenience does not rule, but effectiveness or the potential for effectiveness does. Who are we and what are we trying to do? This is not about denominational standards, but a higher standard. The question is not only "Is this working and should we continue or change" but also "Are we performing in an honorable and holy way?"

6.) *Have a clear, yet changing, sense of mission*

I am not just talking about a pithy mission statement. As one minister said, "There is a Babel of needs." Excellent churches do not try to be all things to all people. They have a vision of where they want to be, and they work toward it. They continually try to discern their place in the community and in the lives of their people, and they are willing to redirect their energies toward what they perceive as their mission, even as it changes.

(7.) *Willingness to break up and reassemble*

When something is not working or a new need arises, excellent churches are ready to put aside old structures and coalitions, even when this includes the sometimes painful disbandment of long-standing church committees or groups that no longer serve the best purposes. These churches operate from perceived need—prayerfully considered—not from entrenched convention—stubbornly maintained. With new groupings, a certain freshness is ever present as new synergies activate and, in the give-and-take of any new adventure, opportunities that might never have surfaced become apparent.

(8.) *Unafraid of being vulnerable and of making mistakes*

The church that doesn't make mistakes, sometimes major mistakes, will never become an excellent church. Excellent churches realize that dreamers and adventurers such as themselves often will go astray, because enthusiasm sometimes does not match the reality of the situation. But when they do make mistakes or strike out in a direction that turns out to be fruitless, they are willing to admit their faults to their congregations—who are used to having human beings not divine beings as their leaders—and go on. To successes, yes. And more mistakes, too.

THE WORK

9 Laity are integral in leadership

Formal training and ordination are not prerequisites for church leadership—competence and a desire to serve, the ability to learn, the humility to admit mistakes, and the courage to stay a difficult course even when conflict arises are the hallmarks of the new generation of lay leaders in excellent churches. These churches recognize the abundance of talent within their congregations—pastoral and business talent, spiritual and physical talent, talent to work with the young and the old and all those in between. With so many gifts showered upon them, these churches readily utilize the abilities of lay people in positions of leadership. "Who can best do this work?" is the question, and when the answer is found, that person is given the opportunity, authority, and support to do the work well.

10 Preach and practice forgiveness and acceptance

Some years ago, while I was doing research for a book, I talked to a professor at a prominent Jewish seminary. He told me that they had trained many great scholars in the past, but now they were changing their focus: to train great rabbis. "Too many of them loved Judaism, but hated Jews," he said. The same is true in our tradition: a love of the power and rich tradition of Christianity, but disdain for sinful, ordinary Christians. This is not so in these excellent churches. There are no hoops to jump through, there is no social ladder to climb in excellent churches. People feel immediately accepted, embraced, and welcomed right now, at this point in their journey of life. It is not a hollow greeting that consists of a generic smile and a handshake upon coming through the doors. It is the deep appreciation for a person's presence, an acknowledgment that everyone is welcome in God's house and that sinners are, in fact, the most welcome. After all, they outnumber everyone else.

(11.)*Believe in evangelizing without "evangelizing"*

Personal contact is the key in excellent churches. Most of the new people brought to these churches come by word of mouth because a coworker, family member, or friend simply told them that they have found a church that truly spoke to their hearts and addressed their needs. This kind of evangelizing has a true integrity; it is not manipulative. It is honest and appealing.

COMMUNITY

(12.)*See themselves as a unique community*

And not as a franchise, either of their denomination or of "Christianity." Excellent churches feel free to innovate, to critique what has gone before them. While they don't see themselves as so unique as to be outside tradition or the larger Christian community, they are a gathering of people unlike any other on earth. They revel in their uniqueness, in the fact that they do not do things the same as everyone else, and in the knowledge that this grouping of people contains talents unrivaled. Excellent churches celebrate this, understanding that there are many paths up the mountain to holiness, and within this group is the freedom to approach God in ways that others may never experience.

(13.)*In transforming the culture, hold government, agencies, and institutions accountable*

All excellent churches see their work as not only serving their constituency but also transforming the world around them. These churches are willing to go into the world and to affect the civic and social structure. They do it out of a biblical mandate and with biblical standards, not merely to be power brokers.

(14.) *Believe in partnerships with other churches, agencies, interest groups, government*

"No church is an island" could be their motto. Excellent churches do not feel they have to do everything by themselves—if they can "outsource," they do it. Excellent churches willingly enter into partnerships that allow them to do their work better. And, when dealing with secular groups, they of course bring special qualities to the mix.

SPIRITUALITY

(15.) *Offer an ascent to God, a relationship*

Theirs is not a social club; something beyond human interaction and companionship is at stake here. Excellent churches provide the tools and the support to forge a real, living, and enduring relationship with the Almighty. Called by many names, the reality is the same: God can be a part of your life, and these churches will help make it so.

(16.) *Traditional without being traditionalist*

Excellent churches are not about reinventing Christianity. They are people of a revered tradition and, if they are members of a denomination, they look back lovingly on its rich history. But their tradition is a beginning, a springboard, not a wall that cannot be breached. Tradition is not a barrier; it is not an excuse not to strike out on another path, uncharted though it may be. They have a sense that they are part of a continuum, that what they may be doing today will also be considered "traditional" in the years ahead.

17. *Bible at their core*

Scripture has the power to instruct, guide, and inspire. Excellent churches have not lost confidence in the bedrock of God's word. They go to it like the thirsty go to a well. This quality pervades both the churches known for their biblically based approach as well as those not known for this emphasis. These churches are introducing the Bible to a new generation of seekers for whom scripture was not part of their upbringing, showing them that this is the kind of wisdom needed for every part of life.

18. *Are innovative about different spiritual approaches*

There are many paths to God and excellent churches realize that the classic ways may not appeal to all seekers. They are not foolish about this and will not merely incorporate the latest "hot" approach, but they are willing to look to other traditions and in other places to find ways to make God concrete in people's lives and readily accessible to them.

19. *Tailor liturgies and programs to different constituencies*

Excellent churches do not believe in the one-size-fits-all approach. They realize that homogeneous groupings of people for worship or study need not be divisive and elitist. They realize that if people are not comfortable, they don't come, so they consciously try to read the needs of various groups and present Christian beliefs and practice within a context each can understand. Theirs is a wide tent, a vast bazaar, and there can be many expressions within.

20. *Have powerful, life-situation preaching*

It is not that the preaching is always of television-performance caliber. But it is always rooted in the practical, in the cries and concerns of normal people. Pastors at excellent churches may be biblical scholars, but they are everyday-life scholars even more. They seek not to impress with their erudition, but with their compassion and understanding.

STRUCTURE

21. Pastors have been in place for years

Excellent churches are products of the Spirit, but they are also products of time. In many denominations—and within the Catholic tradition—there was a propensity or even a policy to move pastors every so many years. The pastor who moves on rarely plumbs the mystery and the real potential of his or her congregation. Changing the manager doesn't always improve the team. Most excellent churches have pastors who have been there for years.

22. Training, training, training

Training is key in excellent churches. They will use local possibilities, but if proper training doesn't already exist, they will create it. They see the church as a seminary. They create training programs that serve the needs of not only their church but their area as well. Training is usually of short duration, with a schedule that fits into a normal person's abilities to attend, and in a convenient location. Some churches share training facilities or arrange consortiums so that churches can design and teach courses in their areas of expertise. Excellent churches send members to workshops and seminars to learn about what is happening in other churches and in such fields as education, psychology, group dynamics, and management.

23. Bring new members to full membership and participation

It is not enough to have a person join a church. Excellent

churches are deliberate about taking new (and existing) members to new levels. They have a specific, usually short program to provide new members with an understanding of what it means to be a modern-day Christian and how they might best serve their church and the world.

24. Call leaders, don't fill slots

Excellent churches are deliberate about leadership, and the pastoral staff is not shy about seeking out people—even though these people may never have offered or seen themselves as leaders—to take on responsibilities. Within every congregation is a great deal of untapped talent, and excellent churches will be sure to claim some of that talent for the Lord's work. Amazingly, they find that people were just waiting to be asked.

25. Break out of their walls and into the world

Excellent churches have no walls, no property lines. They are not secret societies that eschew contact with the world. They are in the marketplace, in civic meetings, in boardrooms, and around water coolers. They realize that there are many people within just a short distance of their doors who will never know about them if they do not reach out into the world.

26. Utilize media well

The Internet, cable television, and print advertising are just some of the ways excellent churches make themselves known and create a link with both homebound members and those who come in person. But these churches are well aware that glitz is not substance, that a mere 800 call to a number on a TV screen may mean little in a person's life if there is no follow-up. There is no substitute for real substance and individual care, and these churches know that well.

Points of
Excellence Index

New points of excellence lead each section, followed by an index to points of excellence that were either noted in a sidebar or can be found within the text.

1. WORSHIP

Superb Children's Ministries

Children's ministries programming is given particularly thoughtful planning at Wilmore Free Methodist Church in a small town near Lexington, Kentucky. The well-developed children's worship program reaches children at their individual levels of understanding through the use of props to dramatize Bible stories. Children are asked to respond to the Bible messages through songs, art, and prayer. The children's music program has choirs, handbells, and chimes for all ages and also teaches music theory. Sunday school, vacation Bible school, the Christian Life Club every Wednesday, Scouts, and other programs all serve children from age two to fifth grade, making Wilmore Free Methodist attractive to young families. The programs are open to member children but serve children in the community, too. "Families are searching for truth and wholesome activities," says Daryl Diddle, director of Christian education. At Wilmore Free Methodist, they can find an abundance of both.

Wilmore Free Methodist Church
1200 North Lexington Road
Wilmore, KY 40390
859-858-3521
www.wfmc.net

BLENDED WORSHIP THAT WORKS

Hours and hours of weekly planning ensure that each Sunday morning worship service is a rich, meaty experience at Evergreen Baptist Church in suburban Los Angeles. "We work a theme through a period of months," says Melvin Fujikawa, the church's full-time worship pastor. "We want to keep it cohesive. It takes a lot of time." Weaving elements such as movie clips, personal testimonies from lay people, and a blend of traditional and contemporary music into the service has resulted in an influx of new people.

Finding a mix of music that appeals to all generations can be a church's greatest challenge—many churches have turned to multiple services with different worship styles to keep both the young and old coming. Evergreen has found the rare balance that works—a blend of traditional hymns, which offer more intellectual lyrics, and contemporary praise choruses that promote an emotional experience. "We like to have the mind and heart linked together," Rev. Fujikawa says. "People are getting the richness of both sides." The pastors get little flack from any generation over the music, which Rev. Fujikawa attributes in part to the church's efforts to foster friendships between the generations through events such as the youth group cooking breakfast for the senior group. "It's relationships that are really key to getting people to accept each other," he says.

The four teaching pastors at Evergreen work closely together to make sure that their sermons are cohesive from week to week and to include elements that will enrich people's learning experience. Realizing that people don't read as much anymore, they often illustrate their sermons with movie clips. For example, during a recent sermon called "Remembering Who We Are," the pastor used a clip from *The Lion King* in which the cub is reminded of his connection with his father. The church also asks lay people to give short testimonies: During this year's Lenten series "Work: Crown or Curse?" members talked about work experiences. "As pastors, we're not there, and it was powerful to have people of faith sharing about their workplace," Rev. Fujikawa says. "It really connected to real life and the practical."

Evergreen Baptist Church
1255 San Gabriel Boulevard
Rosemead, CA 91770
626-280-0477
www.ebcla.org

CHURCH REACHES OUT TO CHURCH

In 1994, to promote racial harmony in Indianapolis, two of the city's largest churches—both with more than one thousand in attendance—shut their doors on a Sunday morning.

Bishop T. Garrison Benjamin of Light of the World Christian Church, a primarily black congregation, and Dr. Bill Enright of Second Presbyterian, a primarily white congregation, had covenanted to establish a sister relationship between their churches. After the traditional pulpit exchange, the congregations rented the largest auditorium in Indianapolis for a joint worship service called "Celebration of Hope" that Sunday morning. There was standing room only.

That service, still held annually, now involves more than forty congregations of many different denominations, and the event has become a movement. The two founding churches now collaborate on an interracial children's choir, a young people's joint service project, three-day spiritual retreats, and a Valentine's Sweetheart dinner. Pastors Benjamin and Enright are now meeting one-on-one with corporate CEOs in Indianapolis to discuss racism and bridge-building in the workplace.

Light of the World Christian Church
5640 East Thirty-eighth Street
Indianapolis, IN 46218
317-547-2273
www.lightoftheworld.org

Second Presbyterian Church
7700 North Meridian Street
Indianapolis, IN 46260
317-253-6461
www.secondchurch.org

SIDEBARS
Refreshing the liturgy: the beginning of church renewal—7
Creativity in worship—26
Life situation preaching—46

Worship is their "front door"—85

Homogeneous groupings; if people are not comfortable, they don't come—114

IN TEXT

Seeker-sensitive, innovative worship—43

Different worship for different groups—65

"Repackaging" the gospel—77

Choir as community—87

Life application preaching—134

Old symbols for a new kind of church—144

2. EDUCATION

Mentoring Young Church Members

When youth become members of Fair Haven Ministries in Hudsonville, Michigan, there is no question that they understand what that means. Every January, junior high– and high school–aged youth who want to join the church enter a six-week mentoring program, a requirement for membership, and they are paired with an adult church member. "It's just a way to really develop these kids and make sure they're ready for the commitment they're making," says Barb Erffmeyer, who works in the program with her husband, Paul. About fifty youth have attended the program each of the four years it's been offered, she says.

The youth and their "guides" meet together for two hours on Sundays to learn the tenets of the faith and the church. Each session integrates teaching with activities the pairs must do together, such as answering questions, making timelines of their lives, and writing together. "It's not just sit and listen and go home," Barb says. "We want to make sure these kids really understand what they learn." Each week the mentor-and-youth pairs do something together outside of church, such as eating out or attending a sporting event, and they also do a Bible study. The friendships that are built between youth and adults often last long beyond the program.

At the end of the six weeks, those youth who decide to join the church turn in a "credo," or a statement of their faith. Creativity is encouraged—youth often express their "credo" in a poem, a song, a dance, or even through woodwork. Six or seven of those are presented at a special Sunday service, where there is "hardly a dry eye" by the end, says Barb. "It really is something that has been very meaningful."

Fair Haven Ministries
2900 Baldwin Street
Hudsonville, MI 49426
616-662-2100
www.fhmin.org

CITYWIDE SEMINARY FOR LEADERSHIP TRAINING

The Greater New Orleans Fellowship School of Ministry is an unadorned, pragmatic training ground for religious leadership. Through three levels of training, both ministers and lay people can learn both the foundation and the practice of biblically based leadership. The first level of training is in the Bible, the second a school of training for Christian education, and the third is more advanced, dealing with counseling, evangelism, and true leadership traits. Any church can send people to the school, and classes are designed to fit into the schedules of working people, not full-time students.

Full Gospel Church of God in Christ
1031 North Claiborne Avenue
New Orleans, LA 70116
504-821-6289
www.fullgospelcogic.com

SIDEBARS

Educating every lay member—*34*

Modular Christian education—*48*

Nine hours to commitment / ministry—*54*

IN TEXT

New visions and roles for lay people—*12, 14*

BYOB (Bring Your Own Bible)—*17*

Cool place for teens—*53*

"High impact" leadership training—*76*

Educating for life during summer camp—*126*

Citywide lay ministry formation—*135*

3. EVANGELIZATION

WELCOMING DAYS

Pastor Charles Brown has moved away from the generic "visitors day" at church to implement a series of welcoming days at Full Gospel. One welcoming day asks congregants to invite their friends, another to ask a neighbor to attend, still another for family members to come with them to church. Coworkers are invited on another Sunday, and another is for all the professional people in congregants' lives—their doctors or teachers or that pharmacist they might see on a regular basis. "It provides people with an excuse to ask somebody to church they might never have asked if it wasn't that specific welcoming day," says Pastor Brown.

Full Gospel Church of God in Christ
1031 North Claiborne Avenue
New Orleans, LA 70116
504-821-6289
www.fullgospelcogic.com

SIDEBARS

Providing necessary support for new satellite churches—75
Effective media; 80 percent come this way—88
Pre-evangelization—112
Sharing life with non-Christians—*maximizing points of contact*—146

IN TEXT

Viewing entire city as mission territory—73
"Islands of hope"; planting churches—74,75
Working with the "tough ones"—79
Ministering in a nonthreatening way—81
Taking evangelization into the world—90
Three steps in evangelization—110
Friendship evangelization—113
Bookstore as entry point—113
Evangelization by personal invitation—145

4. OUTREACH

A "MIDWIFE" CHURCH

Many of Glen Ellyn's community establishments—this Illinois town's first library and kindergarten, a transitional housing center for homeless people, for example—were given birth not by a town council or community vote, but by First Congregational United Church of Christ. The church, which sees itself as a "midwife" to various community organizations, has made a lasting impact on its community by matching its resources with its lay people's visions. "This is our outreach to the community," says Associate Pastor Gloria Hopewell. The church's resources allow community programs to get on their feet—they often then grow into independence.

First Congregational Church encourages members to discern their gifts and put them to work, be that through giving time or money to church or community programs or starting one of their own. The town's transitional housing program, now an independent not-for-profit agency, was originally the idea of a church member who volunteered one hour every week at the local homeless shelter. "They realized there was a big gap between the shelter and permanent housing," Rev. Hopewell says. "It was definitely a need."

Making community service a part of everything from its building plans to its Sunday sermons keeps it a visible priority at the church, which has also founded a pastoral counseling service, a preschool, and a counseling center for troubled youth and their parents. One member who casts movies is linking Glen Ellyn with a church in a troubled area of Chicago. The church's current renovation program includes three sites for developing social service agencies.

First Congregational United Church of Christ
535 Forest Avenue
Glen Ellyn, IL 60137
630-469-3096
www.mmwg.com/fcc-ge

RURAL OUTREACH

In Edison, Georgia, a Baptist church that meets in an old hardware store is proving that there is strength in numbers, even if those numbers are tiny. After a painful split with another church several years ago, this congregation of about twenty-five decided to look for a mission in its community. Members interviewed twenty community members, most of whom cited problems with the local children, many from single-parent homes, who wandered the streets unsupervised after school.

The church now holds summer cookouts, Easter and Christmas events, and a weekly Bible club for children at a trailer park on the outskirts of town. An "Adopt-a-Grandparent" program matches children from the trailer park and local housing project with a senior in the nursing home. "Kids know that there are adults beyond their families who care about them," says Rev. Stacey Simpson, Fellowship Baptist's pastor. "They feel comfortable with us and with our church."

Members, in turn, see children of all races enjoying themselves at church—perhaps a glimpse of a future less entrenched in the racial issues that sometimes divide this town of 1,100. "It has been so meaningful to people here," Rev. Simpson says. "Especially in a small rural community, you have the opportunity to have a bigger impact. Anything that we do here has been huge."

Fellowship Baptist Church
105 South Turner Street
Edison, GA 31746
912-835-2653

MINISTRY OF THE ARTS

Faced with the typical older urban church problems of declining membership, a changing neighborhood, and aging facilities, Pilgrim Congregational Church in Cleveland, Ohio, found a unique way to revive its spirit. The church developed a ministry of the arts that is first-rate. Today, two theater companies and a musical concert ministry group call the church home: Theatre Labyrinth, Kenyetta African Dance Theatre, and Arts Renaissance Tremont. The Theatre Labyrinth company writes its own plays and is known for being gay- and lesbian-friendly. The Kenyetta African Dance Theatre celebrates the African American experience with drama and drums and produces plays by African American writers. In addition, Arts Renaissance Tremont presents free concerts by professional musicians from all over Cleveland, including some members of the Cleveland Symphony.

These groups not only put on their own productions but also routinely assist in Pilgrim's regular worship services, adding a richness and depth to services that attract people from all over the city. The Easter service at Pilgrim was televised nationwide this year, affirming the appeal of its dynamic liturgy. Pastor Laurinda Hafner credits the arts ministry for helping revitalize Pilgrim Congregational. "We used to have rooms that went unused. Now, we've seen so much growth that we use all of our considerable space and may buy the building of another church across the street. The arts ministries have brought people to our church who otherwise might never have come. They may come first for a free concert—but then they feel more willing to come back for a Sunday service."

Pilgrim Congregational United Church of Christ
2592 West Fourteenth Street
Cleveland, OH 44113
216-861-7388

NEWSLETTER REACHES OUT

The congregation of suburban Old Hickory Church of Christ in Tennessee wanted to find a way to reach out to area families. "The idea was to give useful, practical, and encouraging information to families through a newsletter format. The goal is to produce a tool that helps people. If eventually the families realize that Christ has a way to help them—that would be a bonus," says preacher Don Loftis. He edits the newsletter, *Families 2000,* sent every six weeks to families who have requested it or are referred by friends, neighbors, or relatives. With articles about parenting, grandparenting, and marriage, the newsletter is a way for Old Hickory Church of Christ "to let families know that someone in their local community cares about them," he says. Pastor Loftis's wife researches web sites that are geared to family issues, and the newsletter refers families to these resources in a "web site of the month" feature. Recent articles included "Discovering the Secret to Real Happiness," "Coping with Unexpected Crises," and "For Parents: Helping Children Develop Good Self-Esteem."

Families 2000 assures readers that no one will call or come to their door as a result of their free subscription. But they are told that the Old Hickory Church of Christ support prayer ministry will pray for their families by name. The list of families requesting the newsletter is growing, and future plans include offering free seminars and tapes to build stronger family lives.

Old Hickory Church of Christ
1001 Hadley Avenue
Old Hickory, TN 37138
615-847-2386

ALL SPORTSMEN'S DINNER

Begun forty-nine years ago as a way to attract more men to church life at Mount Olivet Lutheran in Minneapolis, Minnesota, the All Sportsmen's Dinner and Round Table today not only brings in men but also a healthy number of women. The annual spring banquet honors one male and one female high school senior athlete of any religion from students nominated from schools across Minnesota. The students nominated must not only excel in two or three sports but also contribute significantly to their communities and churches and be academic achievers. In addition to being specially honored at the dinner attended by about 650 people, each student receives a college scholarship.

Mount Olivet brings in nationally known speakers for the event—past guest speakers include Tom Landry, Lou Holtz, and Mike Ditka. Local Twin Cities teams such as the Vikings, the Wild, and the Twins send contingents of players, coaches, and owners. A high-profile media event, the goal of the dinner and the round table that follows "is to recognize and honor well-rounded, exceptional kids. You hear so many negative stories about youth today—we strive to shine a light on the kids who are doing positive things," says Mount Olivet business manager Tom MacNally. The dinner, held in the church's fellowship hall, is attended by former recipients of the award—who number among them CEOs, doctors, missionaries, and, yes, even professional football players, hockey players, and Olympic-class athletes.

Mount Olivet Lutheran Church
5025 Knox Avenue South
Minneapolis, MN 55419
612-926-7651
www.mtolivet.org

HELPING ONE FAMILY AT A TIME

Once a church predominantly attended by mill workers in the mountain town of Brevard, North Carolina, tiny St. Timothy's is seeing many changes as an influx of retirees make this scenic area their home. When their pastor, Shelly Webb, arrived four years ago, she hoped to encourage this aging congregation to reach out to the community in a significant yet personal way. Through an adult Sunday school class, a Family Partners for Independence team was born. The class was trained to help a "Work First" (North Carolina's program to help get welfare recipients off public assistance) family. "We aren't trying to convert the family; we're trying to be a neighbor," says Rev. Webb. "The training showed us how to respect their rights, encourage them without lecturing, and above all to *listen*." The team's goals are to build the family's self-esteem and help them learn how to achieve financial stability.

The program has benefited not only the family involved but also the church members. "They are discovering their own gifts for ministry through helping this family," Rev. Webb says. "This work helps build a bridge between 'us' and 'them.'"

St. Timothy United Methodist Church
P.O. Box 429
Brevard, NC 28712
828-883-2985
www.gbgm-umc.org/st-tim

MOTHER'S DAY OUT

This Mother's Day Out program in Altus, Oklahoma, is not just a baby-sitting service; it's an evangelism tool. Mona Hunter, the director of children's ministries for Lutheran Ministries of Southwest Oklahoma, has a simple and comprehensive life philosophy: "The solution to problems is ensuring that God is in the middle of everything we do," she says. Mother's Day Out is one way to reach families. When the parents come to pick up their children, Mona talks to them about church and its adult Bible studies. She offers; she does not badger. "I have their attention and they will at least listen. And, happily, we are seeing results in the community. We had eighty percent of the parents at our Christmas program and Bible study. The photographs from our Christmas program are just shocking because of how many people came." The one unchurched family with a child in the program that has started to come to church is just the beginning. Mona acknowledges that the children in the program are not high-risk, but mostly middle-class white kids. "If this were not a means for evangelism, for introducing people to the beauties of a Christian life, it would not be the same."

Lutheran Ministries of Southwest Oklahoma
P.O. Box 368
Lone Wolf, OK 73655
580-846-5459
www.lutheranok.com

THE JESUS CLUB

The thirty-five or so children and teenagers may come to Jesus Club for the free snack, but the staff in Lone Wolf are happy to welcome them, whatever their reason for being there. While the children are taught Bible stories, older students may have a lesson on anything from astronomy to the region's local crops to physics. "The program is an intentional effort to make a difference with these high-risk kids," says Mona Hunter, director of children's ministries. "For these kids, a safe, creative, loving place to play and to learn is exactly what they need—and we focus on that." She uses many creative methods to tell these children about Jesus and God, such as a game where they sit side-by-side, legs extended, and pass an orange to each other without using their hands. If they drop the orange, they have to start again. When the game is over, Mona introduces forgiveness by saying that, like the game, "with Jesus we can start over again when we mess up." Each week Jesus Club leaders also lead the children in small prayer groups, a practice new to many of them. "We pray for a lot of animals," Mona says. "But we don't care what they pray for. We just want them to learn how to talk to God."

Lutheran Ministries of Southwest Oklahoma
P.O. Box 368
Lone Wolf, OK 73655
580-846-5459
www.lutheranok.com

MINISTRY OF STREET PRESENCE

Every Wednesday, in the early evening, six to eight members of All Saints Episcopal Church leave the sanctuary of their sanctuary for a neighborhood "walkabout." They stop in stores and talk to people on the street. They ask about both spiritual and temporal needs. "Is there anything we can do for you?" is their unvarnished offer. Also, they ask what needs or concerns people in the neighborhood might have. "Yes, we heard that there was no place for children to play, so we will work with the neighbors to create a playground, but our walks in our neighborhood have many layers," says the rector, Mark Beckwith. "We just want people to know that we care, we are with them. There are first-time home owners or new businesses—these folks need support. These walks allow us to see how God is already working in our area and how we might respond."

All Saints Episcopal Church
10 Irving Place
Worcester, MA 01609
508-752-3766
www.allsaintschurchworc.org

SIDEBARS

Linking church power to city needs—68
Church–government cooperation—103

IN TEXT

Rural missionary attitude—4
Inserting church into community life—5, 16
Transforming the neighborhood—22, 27
Taking issue with the culture—35, 61
Taking faith into the world—42, 64
Impact family, impact society—47
Liturgy in the streets—62
Sacred bridge between the church and the world—64, 135
Reaching into the neighborhood—79
After conversion, taking belief into their lives—116
College student outreach—119, 127
Volunteer ministry teams—154

5. SPIRITUALITY/INREACH

MEMBERSHIP WEEKEND RETREAT

Membership in some churches, once as easy as walking to the front after a service and telling the pastor you want to join, now often requires membership classes or seminars to ensure that members are clear on what both they and the church believe. The membership program at Chapel Hill Presbyterian in Gig Harbor, Washington, takes that a step further—it wants prospective members to be both educated and involved in friendships with other members. Anyone who wants to join the church is required to attend a weekend retreat and is encouraged to join a small group afterward.

Throughout the weekend, which is held at the church, different pastors give talks about the meaning of being a

Christian, the church's beliefs, the structure of the church's denomination, and the history of the church. Attendees also frequently meet together in small groups, which are encouraged to continue meeting after the weekend. "The retreat becomes a very powerful experience for them because they're going to really develop relationships with people in that group," says Judy Keane, the church's director of communications. "They're really a great way to get below the surface and know other people."

The retreat, which ends with an ice cream social on Sunday night, has become a model for other churches. Pastors from all over Washington have attended the retreat and taken ideas back to their churches, Keane says.

Chapel Hill Presbyterian Church
P.O. Box 829
Gig Harbor, WA 98335
253-851-7779
www.chapelhillpc.org

MINISTERING THROUGH TECHNOLOGY

The phone rarely rings at the office of Warehouse 242 in Charlotte, North Carolina, which is geared toward Generation X, as its technology-savvy congregants are much more apt to communicate electronically. The church also weaves technology into its ministry wherever it can—whether in its cutting-edge web site or the Power Point screens it uses during the church service. The web site, developed by a volunteer church ministry team, is where staff and church attenders post announcements and other information about the church. When the church recently moved to a larger building for its Sunday services, the staff used the web page as the primary means of getting the word out. The easy-to-use page, which is regularly updated, also has a message board for people to post ads for roommates or items they are selling.

Marc Dickmann, Warehouse's pastor of commitment, is building a database of church members and their skills and gifts so that when a member needs help, such as a church member who recently had car problems and couldn't afford the repairs, a database search will identify the mechanics in the church community. "It's sharing resources on a practical level," says Marc, whose job description includes helping people find their spiritual gifts and utilize them in the church community. "I think with this database we'll really see community take shape. We really want to be a community that takes care of itself."

Warehouse 242
1213 West Morehead Street, Suite C
Charlotte, NC 28208
704-344-9242
www.warehouse242.org

MINISABBATICALS TO PREVENT BURNOUT

Burnout is prevalent in pastoral life, and in rural pastoral life it is endemic. To avoid burnout, Bill Geis takes many small trips—two or three days away or even an overnight at a hotel where his kids can swim in the pool—rather than saving up for a big summer vacation. He spends time with his wife each morning over coffee, talking over the day's needs and prioritizing what really needs to be done. Family prayer time at meals and at bedtime are precious; they are occasions to focus on who they are as a family and what this work is really about. "When kids pray, they cut right to the point; I can be pretty scattered sometimes. They bring me back to earth," Bills says. And, like taking his car in for a regular checkup, Bill Geis periodically sees a therapist for a mental tune-up. He tries to love all his parishioners, but spends time with those with whom he has more in common or with those generally simpatico. He looks upon his staff not just as coworkers, but as friends and prayer partners who pray together at least twice a week.

Lutheran Ministries of Southwest Oklahoma
P.O. Box 368
Lone Wolf, OK 73655
580-846-5459
www.lutheranok.com

SIDEBARS

Different approaches to spirituality—63
Need for and use of clerical sabbatical—70
6-point program—Ministry to the whole person—126
Undershepherd Nurturing Ministry—128
Boys II Men program—130
C.pak—a postmodern/biblical small community—148

IN TEXT

Sharing each other's lives—17
Being open with congregants—19
Weekly reports on faith journey—30
Keeping the "edge"—49, 51
Small-group Bible study impact—54
Not just social; a religious commitment—60
Good works, but connected to God—64
Healthy balance between social activism and prayer life—65
Newsletter communication binds group together—118
"Clubs" to increase spiritual growth—119
Practical women's fellowship group—130
Pastor as wounded healer—137

6. ORGANIZATION

SIMPLE CARING

Simple ministries of care—anything from painting a flowerpot for a senior citizen to sending a birthday card to a congregation member—have transformed a Hendersonville, North Carolina, congregation and its relationship with its community. The church's CARE 2000 ministries involve hundreds of church members who both reach out to the community and care for the congregation—the church staff estimates that they contact 3,000 to 3,500 people every month. The church is now planning a third Sunday service to accommodate the resulting growth. "We're just saying 'Hey, we care,'" says Mark Hunnicutt, minister of students, family, and care. "We get a great response—it would blow you away."

Every Sunday, each person at the Sunday service is asked to fill out a CARE 2000 card, so they can indicate any needs they have, prayer requests, and if they prayed to become a Christian. Those cards are then funneled to four CARE 2000 ministry teams, each of which meets one Thursday a month. All team members, who have taken a spiritual gifts test, are matched with a task in the area of inreach, outreach, prayer, hands on, or hospitality that fits his or her gift. Some members write letters to community newcomers, some pray, and others call randomly through the phone book, telling people the church cares. "We're not asking for money, we're not asking for anything," Mark Hunnicutt says. "We're just asking how we can care for you."

Mud Creek Baptist Church
403 Rutledge Drive
Hendersonville, NC 28739
828-692-1262
www.mudcreekchurch.org

OUTREACH THROUGH THE ARTS

Lafayette Avenue Presbyterian Church, in one of Brooklyn's most famous arts havens, has become a presence in its community by melding its missions to the community's personality. Twenty-five years ago, jazz great Eubie Blake occasionally gave free concerts at this church in the Fort Green community, and people would stand on the sidewalks outside the packed church to listen. Today, that program has grown to include cultural arts festivals, dance classes for neighborhood children, and a nationally known, racially integrated gospel choir.

Cultural Crossroads, Inc., which is completely managed by the church but operates legally as a separate entity so it can receive more funding, has given the church a high profile in the community, especially in the past ten years, says Rev. David Dyson. Its weekend-long cultural arts festivals, where artists perform in the church sanctuary, sell their wares in the church gym, and exhibit in the church fellowship hall, attract many people from the community. The church also offers top-quality dance lessons, and scholarships to pay for them, to neighborhood children. "A lot of these kids are poor and couldn't afford to go to a regular dance program," Rev. Dyson says. "They just do wonderful work with these kids."

The arts programs are a common ground for this church and its community, providing plenty of opportunities for what Rev. Dyson calls "indirect evangelism," where people are drawn into the life of the church through their initial involvement in Cultural Crossroads.

Lafayette Avenue Presbyterian Church
85 South Oxford Street
Brooklyn, NY 11217
718-625-7515
www.cloud9.net/~pofn

SIDEBARS

"Growth Council": creative structures outside usual congregational governance—8

Partnership with other small churches and across denominational lines while keeping denominational identity—10

Committed and covenanted—23

Leadership—call them by name—95

Small groups, constantly reorganizing—99

Lay involvement: matching needs with faces—119

Discerning gifts for ministry—155

IN TEXT

Breaking up and forming smaller churches—22

Mission groups to address needs—24

Intentional communities answering a call—25

Acts 2 approach/governance—25, 41, 52

No "ordained" clergy—28

Integrity of membership—28, 33

Communities constantly reformulating—35

Disagree, but stay connected—64

Reorienting a church culture—92

New kind of lay leadership—116

Small groups—117

Stewardship—132

Three bases for a new church—147

Building a leadership culture—154

Index of Excellent Congregations

ALABAMA
Birmingham

MountainTop Community Church
2221 Old Columbiana Road   205-823-7090
Birmingham, AL 35216   www.mountaintopchurch.com

See chapter 3.

Decatur

Calvary Assembly of God
1413 Glenn Street SW   256-355-7440
Decatur, AL 35603   www.calvaryassembly.org

One-year Master's Commission program disciples young adults;
home care groups meet monthly; Sounds of Silence ministry for
deaf and hearing impaired.

Huntsville

First Baptist Church
600 Governors Drive   256-428-9400
Huntsville, AL 35801   www.fbchsv.org

Christian Women's Job Corps assists welfare mothers; sponsors missions on four continents; discipleship/spiritual formation ministries; weekday ministries for children; Sunday services televised in four states.

Mobile

Cottage Hill Baptist Church
4255 Cottage Hill Road   334-660-2422
Mobile, AL 36609   www.cottagehill.org

Many adult and family ministries; outreach ministries include giving quality food and clothing to the needy, prison ministry, and hospital visitation; frequent church-based recreational activities; children's and youth programs.

ALASKA
Fairbanks

First Presbyterian Church
547 Seventh Avenue
Fairbanks, AK 99701   907-452-2406

St. Matthew's Episcopal Church
1030 Second Avenue   907-456-5235
Fairbanks, AK 99701   www.akpub.com/akttt/stmatts

Doors are almost always open, people welcome to drop by to sit and pray; congregation a mix of Western Europeans and Alaskan natives; frequent covered-dish dinners bring together a diverse group of people.

Zion Lutheran Church
2136 McCullam Avenue   907-456-7660
Fairbanks, AK 99701   www.ptialaska.net/~zion

A family-oriented, mission-minded church working in Fairbanks and the Alaskan bush communities; child development center;

college outreach program; participates in many community outreaches, including Fairbanks Rescue Mission.

ARIZONA
Glendale

COMMUNITY CHURCH OF JOY
21000 North Seventy-fifth Avenue   623-561-0500
Glendale, AZ 85308   www.joyonline.org

Seeker-sensitive, family-oriented church provides ministries for all ages, including strong adult, teen, and children's programs; heavy emphasis on family and missions.

Phoenix

FIRST ASSEMBLY OF GOD
13613 North Cave Creek Road   602-867-7117
Phoenix, AZ 85022   www.phoenixfirst.org

More than 200 ministries, including Church on the Street that ministers to street people, the homeless, and prisoners; Evening Star ministry has classes, fellowship, and events for Native American members; Church in the Son biker congregation.

NORTH PHOENIX BAPTIST CHURCH
5757 North Central Avenue   602-707-5757
Phoenix, AZ 85012   www.npbc.org

Scripture-focused worship; contemporary, traditional, and Spanish services incorporate choral and orchestral music; extensive programs for youth; singles ministry; discipleship training.

CALIFORNIA
Alhambra

FIRST EVANGELICAL CHURCH ASSOCIATION
36 West Bay State Street   626-570-8678
Alhambra, CA 91801   www.feca.org

This Chinese-American church uses innovative and holistic means to teach Christian values and truths; extensive outreach ministries.

Aliso Viejo

COAST HILLS COMMUNITY CHURCH
5 Pursuit   949-362-0079
Aliso Viejo, CA 92656   www.coasthillschurch.org

About 3,000 people attend Saturday and Sunday services, which emphasize the creative arts; ministries for all ages include singles, family, and couples ministries; small groups focus on fellowship and service.

Bermuda Dunes

DESERT SPRINGS VINEYARD
79733 Country Club Drive   760-772-8272
Bermuda Dunes, CA 92201   www.dschurch.org

Celebration arts ministry encourages powerful worship; Circle X group connects Gen Xers with God and each other; prayer ministry trains volunteers in intercessory prayer.

Compton

CROSSROADS/NJIA PANDA UNITED METHODIST CHURCH
2354 North Wilmington Avenue
Compton, CA 90222   310-639-3136

Emphasis on women's, men's, and children's ministries; other ministries include new members classes, healing ministry, prayer warriors, hospitality, Bible study, and greeters.

Culver City

CULVER-PALMS UNITED METHODIST CHURCH
4464 Sepulveda Boulevard   310-390-7717
Culver City, CA 90230   www.Hope4LA.org

Thirty-five cultures and countries are represented in this congregation; many Bible study and discipleship opportunities; informal praise and contemporary worship services; Taizé worship and meditative prayer.

Hawthorne

LIGHT AND LIFE COMMUNITY CHURCH
14204 Prairie Avenue
Hawthorne, CA 90250   310-263-2790

Inglewood
FAITHFUL CENTRAL MISSIONARY BAPTIST CHURCH
333 West Florence Avenue
Inglewood, CA 90301   310-330-8000

Predominantly African American megachurch with more than
7,000 members, including many young professionals and college
students; single adult ministry with more than 900 attending
weekly.

Lancaster
DESERT VINEYARD CHRISTIAN FELLOWSHIP
1011 East Avenue I   661-945-2777
Lancaster, CA 93356   www.desertvineyard.org

This suburban, diverse congregation offers many adult education
programs and children's and youth ministries; outreach to rural
Mexican communities; church hosts retreats and ministry training programs at its 320-acre ranch.

Long Beach
LIGHT AND LIFE CHRISTIAN FELLOWSHIP
5951 Downey Avenue   562-630-6074
Long Beach, CA 90805   www.llcf.org

A multicultural healing, equipping, and sending center with
numerous support and recovery groups and new church plants
providing service and leadership opportunities.

Los Angeles
CRENSHAW CHRISTIAN CENTER
7901 South Vermont Avenue   323-758-3777
Los Angeles, CA 90044   www.faithdome.org

This African American megachurch has 17 helps ministries with
a 2,000-member volunteer corps; 32-acre church campus
includes geodesic dome worship center and the Ministry
Training Institute.

FIRST AFRICAN METHODIST EPISCOPAL CHURCH
2270 South Harvard Boulevard   323-730-9180
Los Angeles, CA 90018   www.famechurch.org

A wide variety of programs and projects; Fame Equity Fund assists small minority businesses; six choirs; senior housing; AIDS family housing; forms partnerships with government and businesses to help the community.

IMMANUEL PRESBYTERIAN CHURCH
3300 Wilshire Boulevard
Los Angeles, CA 90010   213-389-3191

Strong children's ministry and social justice programs; this diverse congregation encourages cross-cultural relationships.

MOSAIC
715 South Brady Avenue   323-728-4850
Los Angeles, CA 90022   www.mosaic.org

Reaches out to artists through drama, dance, film, theater, and visual arts; sends out many short- and long-term missionaries; one worship service meets in a downtown nightclub.

WEST ANGELES CHURCH OF GOD IN CHRIST
3045 Crenshaw Boulevard   323-733-8300
Los Angeles, CA 90016   www.westa.org

This large African American church houses a performing arts and counseling center; ministries include multiple choirs, prison outreach, and community development and relations; volunteer services and discipleship training.

YOUNG NAK PRESBYTERIAN CHURCH
1721 North Broadway
Los Angeles, CA 90031   323-227-4093

Ministries for youth, college-age, young adults, and couples; women's and men's prayer groups.

YOUNG SAENG PRESBYTERIAN CHURCH
1829 South Western Avenue
Los Angeles, CA 90006   323-732-7356

Mission Viejo
SADDLEBACK VALLEY COMMUNITY CHURCH
23456 Madero #100   949-581-5683
Mission Viejo, CA 92691   www.saddleback.com

More than 15,000 people have found a home in this communal atmosphere; emphasizes small-group fellowship; extensive classes for children and youth; missions training.

Napa

NAPA FIRST UNITED METHODIST CHURCH
625 Randolph Street
Napa, CA 94559   707-253-1411
    www.napanet.net/organizations/religious/firstmethodist

Five choirs; parish nurse; supports national and international missions projects.

Oakland

ALLEN TEMPLE BAPTIST CHURCH
8501 International Boulevard   510-569-9418
Oakland, CA 94621   www.allen-temple.org

Creative worship and numerous ministries including a leadership institute; housing, services, and activities for seniors; and a church-run credit union; strong Christian education.

Paramount

GRACE PRESBYTERIAN CHURCH
8025 Somerset Boulevard
Paramount, CA 90723   562-633-3964

Pasadena

ALL SAINTS CHURCH
132 North Euclid Avenue   626-796-1172
Pasadena, CA 91101   www.allsaints-pas.org

Peace and justice programs include the coalition for a nonviolent city, which focuses on alleviating violence among youth, family, and communities; C.O.L.O.R.S. program works to overcome racism; Agua Verde Work Team helps a Mexican village.

Poway

LUTHERAN CHURCH OF THE INCARNATION
16889 Espola Road   858-487-2225
Poway, CA 92064   www.lcincarnation.org

Health ministries; Bridge Builders group for adult members; youth and family ministries; congregation supports many area social ministries.

Rosemead

EVERGREEN BAPTIST CHURCH
1255 San Gabriel Boulevard   626-280-0477
Rosemead, CA 91770   www.ebcla.org

Eight-week evangelism programs use open-forum format and contemporary teaching tools; monthly Bible study for recovering drug addicts; diverse worship services include movie clips, testimonies, and worship songs tied to a theme.

San Fransisco

CUMBERLAND PRESBYTERIAN CHINESE CHURCH
865 Jackson Street   415-421-1624
San Francisco, CA 94133   www.Cumberlandsf.org

Tutorial program teaches English and American acculturation to Chinese-speaking immigrants; Saturday night worship service for new immigrants; thriving bilingual youth ministry; weekly senior fellowship attracts more than 250 senior adults.

FIRST CHINESE BAPTIST CHURCH
1-15 Waverly Place   415-362-4139
San Francisco, CA 94108   www.fcbc-sf.org

A bilingual, biracial church committed to ministering to new immigrants and Asian Americans in Chinatown; annual summer youth camp; Friday night school teaches English and citizenship to new immigrants.

GRACE CATHEDRAL
1100 California Street   415-749-6312
San Francisco, CA 94108   www.gracecom.org

Social ministries include feeding the homeless, prison and nursing home ministries, and an annual pilgrimage to Nicaragua; Arts Council oversees art shows in Cathedral galleries; Cathedral Players and Cathedral Singers enhance liturgies.

INGLESIDE PRESBYTERIAN CHURCH
1345 Ocean Avenue
San Francisco, CA 94112   415-587-4472

Community center offers education and employment programs for youth and young adults; thriving church basketball league mentors youth; senior program; boys academy.

SAN FRANCISCO NETWORK MINISTRIES
559 Ellis Street   415-928-6209
San Francisco, CA 94114   www.sfnm.bigstep.com

Reaches out to the poor of San Francisco's Tenderloin neighborhood through evangelism and partnering with existing coalitions; emphasizes direct action for systematic change; church holds memorial services to dignify the deaths of the poor.

ST. PETER'S EPISCOPAL CHURCH
420 Twenty-ninth Avenue
San Francisco, CA 94121   415-751-4942

A vibrant congregation that encourages church involvement through Christ-conscious worship, music, healing, and study; church hosts yoga classes, men's fellowships, and Alcoholics Anonymous and Debtors Anonymous meetings.

San Jose

CHURCH OF THE CHIMES
1447 Bryan Avenue   408-723-3600
San Jose, CA 95118   www.cotconline.org

Offers traditional and contemporary worship services; emphasis on small groups; large young couples group; well-attended Sunday school program; connections groups for children, youth, and adults.

SAN JOSE CHINESE ALLIANCE CHURCH
2360 McLaughlin Avenue   408-280-1021
San Jose, CA 95122   www.sjcac.org

Church oversees Cantonese, English, Mandarin, and Vietnamese congregations; emphasizes civic responsibility; senior center offers evangelistic programs and classes in health, citizenship, exercise, and English; small shepherding groups; youth ministries.

WESLEY UNITED METHODIST CHURCH
566 North Fifth Street   408-295-0367
San Jose, CA 95112   www.gbgm-umc.org/wesleysj

Multiethnic, multicultural, predominantly Japanese-American congregation; ministries for the homeless; vacation Bible school; Bible study groups; Stephen ministry.

San Mateo

COMMUNITY BAPTIST CHURCH
15 South Humboldt Street   650-342-0959
San Mateo, CA 94401   www.community-baptist-church.org

Vibrant youth ministry; English and Cantonese services with Mandarin translation available.

HILLSDALE UNITED METHODIST CHURCH
303 West Thirty-sixth Avenue   650-345-8514
San Mateo, CA 94403   www.gbgm-umc.org/humc4

English and Tongan language worship services; emphasis on family and children's ministries; serves the hungry in the community; senior center; supports related United Methodist denominational ministries.

Santa Ana

CALVARY CHAPEL
3800 South Fairview Road   714-979-4422
Santa Ana, CA 92704   www.calvarychapel.com/costamesa

Services and fellowship groups for many diverse ethnic groups; adult and children's developmentally disabled ministries; several men's Bible study and prayer groups.

Santa Barbara

FREE METHODIST CHURCH OF SANTA BARBARA
1435 Cliff Drive
Santa Barbara, CA 93109   805-965-1338
                www.west.net/ucx/mthodist/churches.html

Cliff Drive Care Center weekday ministry serves children,

youth, adults, parents, and seniors; counseling center; extensive youth program; leadership training center.

Santa Monica

FIRST UNITED METHODIST CHURCH
1008 Eleventh Street   310-393-8258
Santa Monica, CA 90403   www.santamonicaumc.org

See chapter 6.

Solana Beach

SOLANA BEACH PRESBYTERIAN CHURCH
120 Stevens Avenue   858-509-2580
Solana Beach, CA 92075   www.solanapres.org

Alpha program for people interested in learning more about Christianity; Discovering ministry helps members identify and put into practice their spiritual gifts and passions; adult members tutor Hispanic children weekly with schoolwork and English.

Torrance

TORRANCE FIRST PRESBYTERIAN CHURCH
1880 Crenshaw Boulevard
Torrance, CA 90501   310-618-2222

Vacaville

ST. PAUL'S UNITED METHODIST CHURCH
101 West Street
Vacaville, CA 95688   707-448-5154

Despite its tiny size, this church has a large impact on its community through many outreaches, including a food bank, thrift store, and annual bike-a-thon.

Van Nuys

THE CHURCH ON THE WAY
14300 Sherman Way   818-779-8000
Van Nuys, CA 91405   www.tcotw.org

Many home-based small groups; ministries for single adults, married couples, young adults, youth, and seniors; several choirs and orchestras; monthly men's ministry.

COLORADO
Aurora

THE VINEYARD ON SMOKY HILL ROAD
20050 East Smoky Hill Road   303-690-2520
Aurora, CO 80015   www.vineyardsmokyhill.org

Emphasizes equipping and training lay people for ministry; tri-annual "Make a Connection Sunday" links people to small groups and dinner fellowships; church expresso bar encourages fellowship; sports teams; youth and children's ministries.

Colorado Springs

FIRST PRESBYTERIAN CHURCH
219 East Bijou Street   719-471-3763
Colorado Springs, CO 80903   www.first-pres.org

Young adult ministries include seekers group for college-age and ministry for Gen-X singles; workshops for divorce, recovery, grief, and relationships; dynamic music ministry with a blend of musical styles; a choir and 10-piece band at all services.

NEW LIFE CHURCH
11025 Highway 83   719-594-6602
Colorado Springs, CO 80921   www.newlifechurch.org

Extensive ministries to youth of all ages draw thousands each week; more than 500 small groups are integral to church life here; worship team innovates through bands, choirs, and special music events.

Denver

MONTVIEW BOULEVARD PRESBYTERIAN CHURCH
1980 Dahlia Street   303-355-1651
Denver, CO 80220   www.montview.org

Outstanding music program offers choirs for all ages; adult education program includes lectures, retreats, and seminars; children's education explores the Bible through movies, computer, drama, art, and games; annual youth work trip.

OUR SAVIOR'S LUTHERAN CHURCH
915 East Ninth Street
Denver, CO 80218   303-831-7023

Church operates as a neighborhood ministry center, providing senior citizen housing, food and clothing distribution, and care for the mentally ill; partners with other local churches for social action; two Sunday services offer several styles of worship.

RIVERSIDE BAPTIST CHURCH
2401 Alcott   303-433-8665
Denver, CO 80211   www.riversidebaptist.com

See chapter 5.

ST. BARNABAS EPISCOPAL CHURCH
1280 Vine Street
Denver, CO 80206   303-388-6469

Fort Collins
VINEYARD CHRISTIAN FELLOWSHIP-FORT COLLINS
1201 Riverside Avenue   970-484-5999
Fort Collins, CO 80524   www.vineyardfc.org

Lafayette
DISCOVERY CHRISTIAN CHURCH
385 South Pierce Avenue, Unit D   303-604-6280
Louisville, CO 80027   www.discovery-church.org

Growing suburban church emphasizes arts in Sunday worship, including drama and multimedia presentations; small groups; strong children's and youth programs; women's ministries.

Niwot
ROCKY MOUNTAIN CHRISTIAN CHURCH
9447 Niwot Road   303-652-2211
Niwot, CO 80503   www.rmcc.org

Growing church of more than 2,000; relevant, biblical preaching; nonauditional choir has 150 members; annual Christmas choir program is a community event; strong student ministry; adult small groups.

Security

ISRAELITE CHURCH OF GOD IN CHRIST
123 Security Boulevard   719-392-3322
Security, CO 80911   www.csprings.com/church/pow309.htm

Wheat Ridge

THE NEXT LEVEL CHURCH
4980 Kipling Street, Suite 14   303-422-3777
Wheat Ridge, CO 80033   www.tnl.org

This postmodern church's weekly Tuesday night services attract a
large, unchurched crowd; small groups provide life for people
searching for community; comprehensive approach to worship
includes musical worship, reflection, and prayer.

CONNECTICUT

Essex

ST. JOHN'S EPISCOPAL CHURCH
Main Street and Cross Street
Essex, CT 06426   860-767-8095

Newington

GRACE EPISCOPAL CHURCH
124 Maple Hill Avenue   860-666-3331
Newington, CT 06111   www.gracechurchnew.org

Growing church offers both contemporary and traditional worship services; strong Lenten series provides educational experiences; frequent fellowship dinners are well attended.

South Glastonbury

CONGREGATIONAL UNITED CHURCH OF CHRIST
16 High Street
South Glastonbury, CT 06073   860-633-4651

DISTRICT OF COLUMBIA

LUTHER PLACE MEMORIAL LUTHERAN CHURCH
1226 Vermont Avenue NW
Washington, D.C. 20005   202-667-1377

This inner-city church works for systematic change, focusing on
homeless women; Luther Place complex, where more than

1,200 volunteers work, offers hospitality, recovery programs, and affordable housing.

NEW YORK AVENUE PRESBYTERIAN CHURCH
1313 New York Avenue NW   202-393-3700
Washington, D.C. 20005   www.nyapc.org

Priority to serve the elderly, children, mentally ill, and the homeless; after-service refreshments provide weekly fellowship; extensive adult education classes; community outreach; meals on wheels; many support and recovery groups.

ST. COLUMBA'S
4201 Albemarle Street   202-363-4119
Washington, D.C. 20016   www.columba.org

Numerous youth programs, choirs, and educational groups; outreach programs include Christmas in April to assist elderly inner-city residents with home repairs and tutoring for at-risk children; transitional program for women.

SEEKERS CHURCH
278 Carroll Street NW   202-829-9882
Washington, D.C. 20012   www.seekerschurch.org

See chapter 2.

SHILOH BAPTIST CHURCH
1500 Ninth Street NW   202-232-4200
Washington, D.C. 20001   www.shilohbaptist.org

Christian education ministry addresses holistic needs of the church community and promotes the African American perspective in church programs; ministries include leadership development, communications, evangelism, social justice, and financial services.

FLORIDA
Clearwater

ST. JOHN'S EPISCOPAL CHURCH
1676 South Belcher Road   727-531-6020
Clearwater, FL 33764   www.stjohns-online.org

Emphasizes priesthood of believers; children's ministry; spiritual growth retreats and guidance; thrift shop; Eager Beavers group maintains church buildings and grounds.

Fort Lauderdale

CORAL RIDGE PRESBYTERIAN CHURCH
5555 North Federal Highway   954-771-8840
Fort Lauderdale, FL 33308   www.crpc.org

The media ministry of this 9,000-member church reaches thousands nationwide through TV, radio, the Internet, and printed materials; many adult ministries; church concert series draws nationally known artists; assimilation ministry welcomes newcomers.

FLAMINGO ROAD BAPTIST CHURCH
12401 Stirling Road
Fort Lauderdale, FL 33330   954-434-1500

Jacksonville

FIRST BAPTIST CHURCH
124 West Ashley Street   904-356-6077
Jacksonville, FL 32202   www.fbcjax.com

Christian Life University with classes on a wide range of Christian topics; School of Music for all ages; worship services broadcast on radio and TV.

Lake Placid

FIRST PRESBYTERIAN CHURCH
118 North Oak Street
Lake Placid, FL 33852   863-465-2742

Thriving ministries for youth and children; worship ministries include several choirs, liturgical dance, and drama teams; emphasizes involvement in community outreach.

Lake Wales

FIRST PRESBYTERIAN CHURCH
16 North Third Street
Lake Wales, FL 33853   863-676-0711

Lakeland

SHEPHERD ROAD PRESBYTERIAN CHURCH
1217 Shepherd Road   863-646-3219
Lakeland, FL 33811   www.srpc.net

Three Sunday services and many ministry teams, including
financial, compassion, emergency preparedness, greeters/ush-
ers, library, prayer, and recreation; well-organized prayer chain;
strong youth and children's programs.

Leesburg

FIRST BAPTIST CHURCH
220 North Thirteenth Street   352-787-1005
Leesburg, FL 34748   www.fbcleesburg.org

More than 3,000 attend weekly; emphasizes lay ministry and
ministry evangelism; ministry village includes rescue mission for
men, women's shelter, pregnancy care center, children's rescue
center, teen home, furniture barn, and food pantry.

Melbourne

TABERNACLE CHURCH
1619 Ferndale Avenue   321-259-2024
Melbourne, FL 32935   www.tabernacle.net

Family and Singles Life Center offers classes, pastoral care, and
activities; Freedom group for seekers ages 18 and up; home
groups; Joy ministry for people over 50; youth groups.

Pensacola

BROWNSVILLE ASSEMBLY OF GOD
3100 West Desoto Street   850-433-3078
Pensacola, FL 32505   www.brownsville-revival.org

A revival has been active here since 1995; cell groups; large
youth ministry with three youth pastors; strong children's worship; discipleship programs for adults and youth.

Venice

ST. MARK'S EPISCOPAL CHURCH
508 Riviera Street
Venice, FL 34285   941-488-7714

GEORGIA
Atlanta

BEN HILL UNITED METHODIST CHURCH
2099 Fairburn Road   404-344-0618
Atlanta, GA 30331   www.benhill-umc.com

Large African American congregation has a strong music focus
with nine choirs; men's outreach; extensive youth programs;
three Sunday worship services and youth church; full-time preschool program; church takes a holistic approach to ministry.

BIG BETHEL A.M.E. CHURCH
220 Auburn Avenue NE   404-659-0248
Atlanta, GA 30303   www.bigbethelame.org

Numerous outreach programs include Homeless Intervention
and Prevention Project and counseling for at-risk children;
Andrew ministry teaches sharing one's faith without fear; children's ministry; active singles ministry; dance ministry.

CENTRAL PRESBYTERIAN CHURCH
201 Washington Street SW   404-659-0274
Atlanta, GA 30303   www.centralpresbyterianatl.org

This church's extensive outreach ministries include an outreach
center and work with homeless families; Central Neighbors program divides the congregation into small parishes to enhance
pastoral care; choirs and education ministries for all ages.

PEACHTREE PRESBYTERIAN
3434 Roswell Road NW   404-842-5800
Atlanta, GA 30305   www.peachtreepres.org

One of the largest Presbyterian churches in America; pastoral
counseling center; midweek alternative worship service; large
singles ministry; extensive youth involvement; support and
recovery groups.

ST. PHILIP A.M.E. CHURCH
240 Candler Road SE   404-371-0749
Atlanta, GA 30317   www.saintphilip.org

Inviting African American congregation has several choirs; prison ministry; child development center; outreach to the homeless; dance ministry.

TRINITY PRESBYTERIAN CHURCH
3003 Howell Mill Road NW   404-237-6491
Atlanta, GA 30327   www.trinityatlanta.org

New music center brings multigenerational members together for arts festivals and concerts; many small groups, including groups for seniors, young adults, and young families.

WORLD CHANGERS
2500 Burdett Road   770-907-9490
College Park, GA 30349   www.worldchangers.org/wcci_t.htm

African American congregation of more than 20,000 offers a variety of programs, including an athletic ministry, business network, marriage counseling, and several choirs; outreach to nursing homes; performing arts ministry; extensive media services.

Columbus

ST. LUKE UNITED METHODIST CHURCH
1104 Second Avenue   706-327-4343
Columbus, GA 31901   www.stlukeum.com

Offers a variety of ministries for families; small groups; men's and women's ministries; respite care ministry provides temporary relief for caregivers and programs for the elderly; many music ministries; sports teams; counseling services; art gallery.

Decatur

OAKHURST BAPTIST CHURCH
222 East Lake Drive   404-378-3677
Decatur, GA 30030   www.oakhurstbaptist.org

Music and youth ministries; Sunday church school for all ages; mission groups; drug and alcohol recovery program for homeless men; church has started many thriving ministries, including Baptist Peace Fellowship of North America.

OAKHURST PRESBYTERIAN CHURCH
118 Second Avenue
Decatur, GA 30030   404-378-6284

Multiracial congregation with community ministries including tutoring, senior services, youth arts academy, and prison ministry; antiracism and social justice ministries have received national attention.

RAY OF HOPE CHRISTIAN CHURCH
2778 Snapfinger Road   770-696-5100
Decatur, GA 30034   www.rayofhope.org

Hosts Bible study and breakfast and provides transportation to Sunday service for homeless men; employment ministry provides jobs for youth and adults through quarterly job fairs; emphasis on evangelism and the arts in worship; extensive youth programs.

Doraville

YOUNG-NAK PRESBYTERIAN CHURCH
3100 Oakcliff Road
Doraville, GA 30340   770-936-2800

Edison

FELLOWSHIP BAPTIST CHURCH
105 South Turner Street
Edison, GA 31746   912-835-2653

Tiny church has made a large impact on its community; ministers to local trailer park, including Bible clubs for children who live there and summer Sunday cookouts with children and their families; many seasonal children's activities.

Lithonia

NEW BIRTH MISSIONARY BAPTIST CHURCH
6400 Woodrow Road   770-696-9600
Lithonia, GA 30038   www.newbirth.org

African American congregation provides substance-abuse ministry, GED classes, tutoring, family life center, health services and outreach to homebound; choral and orchestral groups; youth ministry.

Savannah
St. Paul CME Church
1601 Barnard Street
Savannah, GA 31401   912-233-2849

Focus on strengthening families morally and spiritually; school
for boys provides mentoring and stresses Christian identity;
community ministries include food distribution and drug abuse
recovery program; neighborhood revitalization.

HAWAII
Ewa Beach
Hope Chapel Kapolei
91-902 Fort Weaver Road, Suite 105   808-689-8328
Ewa Beach, HI 96706   www.hopechapelkapolei.org

This church is structured around Minichurches, home-based
small groups led by trained lay pastors; emphasizes church planting and training potential pioneer pastors; children's church;
services on Friday night, Sunday morning and evening.

IDAHO

Boise
Vineyard of Boise
4950 North Bradley Street   208-377-1477
Boise, ID 83714   www.vcfboise.org

Emphasis on men's, women's, and children's ministries; extensive classses on the basics of Christianity, discipleship, the Bible,
and theology.

Twin Falls
First Church of the Nazarene
1231 Washington Street North   208-733-6610
Twin Falls, ID 83301   www.tfnaz.com

Celebration worship ministries include choirs for children and
adults, orchestra, praise teams, bands, drama, production, and
technical teams; numerous adult and youth small groups; thriving ministries for seniors, youth, and children.

ILLINOIS
Arlington Heights

ST. PETER LUTHERAN CHURCH
111 West Olive Street   847-259-4114
Arlington Heights, IL 60004   www.stpeter-ah.org

Thriving Christian school; youth ministry has two Bible studies a week and outreach events; many community outreaches; strong worship teams.

Chicago

CHINESE CHRISTIAN UNION CHURCH
2301 South Wentworth Avenue   312-842-8545
Chicago, IL 60616   www.ccuc.net

See chapter 7.

CORNELL BAPTIST CHURCH
5001 South Ellis Avenue
Chicago, IL 60615   773-268-4910

FOURTH PRESBYTERIAN CHURCH
126 East Chestnut Street   312-787-4570
Chicago, IL 60611   www.fourthchurch.org

Traditional yet accessible worship with quality music; vesper service with Communion; mission outreach tutors hundreds of children from nearby housing projects; adult education initiative with Bible, theological studies, and social issues.

LA CAPILLA DEL BARRIO / THE NEIGHBORHOOD CHAPEL
3058 West Armitage Avenue
Chicago, IL 60647   773-227-4673

Mentoring and tutoring program matches at-risk youth with responsible adults; street ministry in drug- and gang-infested neighborhood; active prayer network.

RAVENSWOOD FELLOWSHIP UNITED METHODIST CHURCH
4511 North Hermitage Avenue
Chicago, IL 60640   773-561-2610

ST. EDMUND EPISCOPAL CHURCH
6105 South Michigan Avenue
Chicago, IL 60637   773-288-0038

Church-sponsored community school; community development corporation offers many affordable housing units; rich
worship services mix Episcopalian tradition and African
American culture; church leaders stay connected with city offi-
cials and agencies.

TRINITY UNITED CHURCH OF CHRIST
400 West Ninety-fifth Street   773-962-5650
Chicago, IL 60628   www.tucc.org

Center for African Bible Studies offers between 20 and 25 classes
weekly; many youth ministries—including dance programs,
tutoring, and athletic programs—serve more than 1,000 children; five choirs, including 280-member sanctuary choir.

Decatur

MARANATHA ASSEMBLY OF GOD
555 West Imboden Drive   217-423-2452
Decatur, IL 62521   www.maranatha-assembly.org

Growing multicultural church offers ministries for all life circumstances; active and extensive homeless outreach; children's
ministries include day care, preschool, and inner-city outreach.

Downers Grove

FIRST CONGREGATIONAL CHURCH
1047 Curtiss Street   630-968-0358
Downers Grove, IL 60516   www.firstcongdg.org

Excellent worship includes eight choirs and Taizé services;
homeless shelter; church manages the longest-running coffeehouse in the Chicago suburbs; preschool for 2-year-olds through
kindergarten.

FIRST PRESBYTERIAN CHURCH
Fourth Street and Fairview Avenue   630-968-5432
Downers Grove, IL 60515   www.iit.edu/~bradrob/cs460

Blended worship sevices mix traditional and contemporary styles; a variety of groups for youth and adults build faith and fellowship; many family activities, including churchwide picnic and weeklong summer camp.

Evanston

IMMANUEL LUTHERAN CHURCH
616 Lake Street   847-864-4464
Evanston, IL 60201   www.forministry.com/churchsearch.asp

Lively but traditional liturgical worship; scholarly preaching on biblical texts; many hands-on social ministry projects; intergenerational social activities.

Glen Ellyn

FIRST CONGREGATIONAL UNITED CHURCH OF CHRIST
535 Forest Avenue   630-469-3096
Glen Ellyn, IL 60137   www.mmwg.com/fcc-ge

Innovative children's and youth ministries; encourages lay people to put faith into action; supports housing programs and developing community organizations; strong worship ministry.

ST. THOMAS UNITED METHODIST CHURCH
2 South 511, Route 53
Glen Ellyn, IL 60137   630-469-1214
                        www.members.tripod.com/st-thomas-umc

Suburban congregation supports many community groups, including CROP walk, food pantry, and Aurora Day Care; mission projects to Zaire and Appalachia; Bible study share groups; healing services; numerous fellowship outings.

Glenview

GLENVIEW COMMUNITY CHURCH
1000 Elm Street   847-724-2210
Glenview, IL 60025   www.gccucc.org

Supports national and global missions projects; multiple choirs; rotational model church school programs; active high school youth programs; full adult education; parish nurse; nursery school; interfaith services; seniors programs; pastoral care teams.

Mundelein

FAITH LUTHERAN CHURCH
1966 West Hawley Street
Mundelein, IL 60060   847-566-8941

Postmodern, Generation-X focus; programs for growing Mexican population; Alpha course for exploring the Christian faith.

Orland Park

ORLAND PARK CHRISTIAN CHURCH
7500 West Sycamore Drive   708-532-4900
Orland Park, IL 60462   www.opcrc.org

Ministries to the disabled include rest and caring ministries for the elderly, children with special needs and their caregivers; children's ministry; many adult education classes and support groups.

Peoria

FIRST UNITED METHODIST CHURCH OF PEORIA
116 NE Perry Avenue   309-673-3641
Peoria, IL 61603   www.fumcpeoria.org

Large congregation known for its prayer ministry; outreach to urban area includes food ministry; numerous choirs and bands; children's choir school.

South Barrington

WILLOW CREEK COMMUNITY CHURCH
67 East Algonquin Road   847-765-5000
South Barrington, IL 60010   www.willowcreek.org

One of America's largest churches, this seeker-sensitive congregation is multicultural and multigenerational; many small groups; contemporary service for Gen Xers; opportunities for handicapped and developmentally challenged.

Washington

FAITH CHRISTIAN CENTRE
2354 Hollands Grove Road   309-745-9376
Washington, IL 61571   www.faithchristiancentre.org

Madhouse ministry reaches out to junior high students; Planet ministry for older teens has its own band, drama team, and web site; Shekinah works with young adults offering Life groups, retreats, and mission trips.

Wauconda
MESSIAH LUTHERAN CHURCH
25225 West Ivanhoe Road   847-526-7161
Wauconda, IL 60084   www.messiah-wauconda.org

Preschool ministries reach out to the community; care for children before and after school; large music ministry for children and adults.

INDIANA
Indianapolis
LIGHT OF THE WORLD CHRISTIAN CHURCH
5640 East Thirty-eighth Street   317-547-2273
Indianapolis, IN 46218   www.lightoftheworld.org

Large African American church is committed to education and excellence; Project Impact Indianapolis works with court-referred, first-offender teens; hosts an ecumenical program to promote racial respect between pastors and congregations.

ST. LUKE'S UNITED METHODIST CHURCH
100 West Eighty-sixth Street   317-846-3404
Indianapolis, IN 46260   www.stlukesumc.com

Three handbell choirs and five vocal choirs add a delightful element to traditional worship; "The Garden," an innovative Bible study program, is designed to help people grow spiritually.

SECOND PRESBYTERIAN CHURCH
7700 North Meridian Street   317-253-6461
Indianapolis, IN 46260   www.secondchurch.org

Megachurch with a two-year program for seminary graduates that offers hands-on learning in parish ministry; cofounder of Celebration Hope, 60 churches that meet annually for a city-wide worship service; Sunday evening worship features a jazz trio.

South Bend

St. Michael and All Angels Episcopal Church
53720 North Ironwood Road
South Bend, IN 46635   219-243-0632

Ministry of friendliness and hospitality reaches out to both
members and newcomers; strong ministries for children to college age.

Zionsville

Zionsville Presbyterian Church
4775 West 116th Street   317-873-6503
Zionsville, IN 46077   www.zpc.org

IOWA
Des Moines

First Assembly of God
2725 Merle Hay Road   515-279-9766
Des Moines, IA 50310   www.dsm1ag.org

Reaches out to many different ethnic groups; "Rock the City"
works with teens for spiritual growth; innovative Pulse worship
services for young adults.

Meredith Drive Reformed Church
5128 Meredith Drive   515-276-4901
Des Moines, IA 50310   www.MDRC.net

Large suburban church offers blended, participatory worship;
children's Sunday school uses small-group model; youth ministry emphasizes personal relationships; many small groups and
music ministries.

Plymouth Congregational Church
4126 Ingersoll Avenue   515-255-3149
Des Moines, IA 50312   www.plymouthchurch.com

Women's fellowship and Bible study groups; artists display work
in sanctuary; mentoring programs; support and recovery
groups; several choirs; yoga classes.

Pella

THIRD REFORMED CHURCH
708 East Thirteenth Street   641-628-3051
Pella, IA 50219   www.trcpella.com

Emphasis on helping congregants discover their spiritual gifts and use them for service; cell groups; extensive children's and youth programs.

KANSAS
Shawnee Mission

LAO AMERICAN CHURCH
9237 Noland Road
Shawnee Mission, KS 66213   913-541-0800

KENTUCKY
Louisville

CANAAN MISSIONARY BAPTIST CHURCH
2840 Hikes Lane   502-459-5578
Louisville, KY 40216   www.canaanbaptist.com

Holistic rites of passage program for boys and girls; young adult ministry nurtures relationships and promotes sense of self, family, and community; drama ministry enriches worship.

SOUTHEAST CHRISTIAN CHURCH
920 Blankenbaker Parkway   502-253-8000
Louisville, KY 40243   www.southeastchristian.org

This megachurch with 17,000 members offers blended worship with Bible-based preaching, drama, special music, and praise choruses; hundreds of volunteers serve as greeters for Sunday services; 15 percent of budget goes to missions.

Owensboro

OWENSBORO CHRISTIAN CHURCH
2818 New Hartford Road   270-683-2706
Owensboro, KY 42303   www.owensborochristian.org

Church-run halfway house for drug addicts and alcoholics; excellent music; telecare ministry calls each member monthly asking for prayer requests; 12-week evangelism training program.

Wilmore

WILMORE FREE METHODIST CHURCH
1200 North Lexington Road   859-858-3521
Wilmore, KY 40390   www.wfmc.net

Consistently excellent preaching, music, and drama because of close proximity to seminary; comprehensive children's programming attracts young families; generous and friendly congregation.

LOUISIANA
Baton Rouge

CHURCH OF THE HOLY SPIRIT
14344 South Harrell's Ferry Road
Baton Rouge, LA 70816   225-751-2116
          www.episcopalian.org/hspirBLA/CHS.html

Church members and volunteers tend four-acre, church-owned garden to raise fruits, vegetables, and fish, which are donated to Baton Rouge's Missionary Sisters of Charity; video school for short-term missions training; Stephen ministry; prison ministry.

Kenner

VINEYARD CHRISTIAN FELLOWSHIP-KENNER
4224 Williams Boulevard
Kenner, LA 70065   504-467-3257

High-energy children's programs provide a good balance of relationships, fun, and spiritual development; Alpha course for unchurched and new believers; 40 percent of regular attenders involved in small groups.

Lake Charles

GLAD TIDINGS CHURCH
3400 Texas Street   318-477-7774
Lake Charles, LA 70607   www.gladtidingschurch.org

Dynamic praise and worship; altar calls and emphasis on evangelism; thriving discipleship program helps new believers plug into church ministry.

New Orleans

CENTRAL CONGREGATIONAL UNITED CHURCH OF CHRIST
2401 Bienville Avenue
New Orleans, LA 70119   504-822-3223

Family Life Enrichment Center provides a variety of counseling services; strong youth programs.

FRANKLIN AVENUE BAPTIST CHURCH
2515 Franklin Avenue   504-947-2408
New Orleans, LA 70117   www.franklinabc.com

Brotherhood ministry helps men over 18 become positive role models; Nurses Guild provides health education; witnessing outreach ministry seeks to spread the gospel.

FULL GOSPEL CHURCH OF GOD IN CHRIST
1031 North Claiborne Avenue   504-821-6289
New Orleans, LA 70116   www.fullgospelcogic.com

See chapter 8.

GREATER ST. STEPHEN'S FULL GOSPEL BAPTIST CHURCH
9661 Lake Forest Boulevard   504-244-6800
New Orleans, LA 70127   www.greaterststephen.org

Worship services held at three locations citywide; discipleship training available; WORD EXPLOSION offers a condensed worship focused on "hot" topics.

RAYNE MEMORIAL UNITED METHODIST CHURCH
3900 St. Charles Avenue   504-899-3431
New Orleans, LA 70115   www.gbgm-umc.org/rayne

Outreach ministries include transitional housing program, partnership with a local elementary school and soup kitchen; strong music program; Sunday school for all ages; singles ministry.

MAINE
Palmyra

ST. MARTIN'S EPISCOPAL CHURCH
P.O. Box 107
Palmyra, ME 04965   207-938-4414

This small rural church offers literacy, GED preparation, and basic computer skill programs for adults; hosts about 25 public suppers annually; supports local food bank.

Portland

WILLISTON-WEST CHURCH, UCC

32 Thomas Street   207-774-4060
Portland, ME 04102   www.geocities.com/willistonweb

Promotes lay involvement in worship and community life; open and affirming to all people; outreach programs to local areas and to Bedouin children in Palestine.

MARYLAND
Baltimore

BETHEL A.M.E. CHURCH

1300 Druid Hill Avenue   410-523-4273
Baltimore, MD 21217   www.bethel1.org

Outreach Center helps people dealing with poverty, teen pregnancy, and homelessness; Bethel Christian School for elementary-age children; dance ministry; strong men's ministry; pastor's sermons broadcast to 130 countries.

MADISON AVENUE PRESBYTERIAN CHURCH

2110 Madison Avenue
Baltimore, MD 21217   410-523-7935

Works for major community redevelopment in Baltimore through small and large projects; child development center; rebuilds neighborhood housing; partners with other organizations and churches for urban ministry.

NEW SONG COMMUNITY CHURCH

1385 North Gilmore Street
Baltimore, MD 21217   410-728-7725

A multiracial congregation dedicated to community development in Sandtown; works with other organizations to provide housing and health care for low-income families; job search and counseling services; learning center and school; arts and media programs.

PAYNE MEMORIAL A.M.E. CHURCH
1714 Madison Avenue   410-669-8739
Baltimore, MD 21217   www.payne-ame.org

This thriving African American church focuses on innovative, holistic ministries for families; church's nonprofit agency sponsors many programs for children and youth as well as initiatives addressing the community's housing and employment needs.

MASSACHUSETTS
Boston
BOSTON CHINESE EVANGELICAL CHURCH
249 Harrison Avenue   617-426-5711
Boston, MA 02111 www.ifcss.org/ftp-pub/org/bcec

Many small fellowships and Bible study groups for all ages; after school programs; ESL classes; middle school summer day camp; supports many social ministries.

Brookline
CHINESE CHRISTIAN CHURCH OF NEW ENGLAND
1835 Beacon Street
Brookline, MA 02445   617-232-8652

Biweekly Bible study; seeker-friendly with many students and professionals from China; two clergy rotate preaching with lay ministers from the congregation and guest preachers.

Dorchester
AZUSA CHRISTIAN COMMUNITY
411 Washington Street
Dorchester, MA 02124   617-822-0335

Ten-point plan outlines ways a church can stop violence; oversees Ella J. Baker House, which serves thousands of inner-city youth; founded National Ten Point Leadership Foundation.

Worcester
ALL SAINTS EPISCOPAL CHURCH
10 Irving Place   508-752-3766
Worcester, MA 01609 www.allsaintschurchworc.org

See chapter 4.

MICHIGAN
Detroit

HARTFORD MEMORIAL
18700 James Couzens Freeway
Detroit, MI 48235   313-861-1300

MESSIAH EPISCOPAL CHURCH
231 East Grand Boulevard   313-567-1158
Detroit, MI 48207   www.comnet.org/local/orgs/messiah

Focus on inner-city community development; outreach programs include housing corporation, young leadership development, senior citizens ministries, women's outreach, and health and fitness; drama and prayer teams; youth programs.

ST. ANDREW-REDEEMER LUTHERAN CHURCH
2261 Marquette Avenue
Detroit, MI 48208   313-896-3370

Rich worship life includes elements from African American, German, and Laotian cultures; works with churches and community organizations to attract industry and jobs to the neighborhood; Community Center Ministry offers HIV testing and a meals program.

Farmington Hills

ORCHARD UNITED METHODIST CHURCH
30450 Farmington Road   248-626-3620
Farmington Hills, MI 48334   www.orchardumc.org

Strong family-based worship; choral music is a delightful addition to traditional services; Dinners for Eight provide forums for congregants to meet and fellowship.

Grand Rapids

CALVARY CHURCH
777 East Beltline Avenue NE   616-956-9377
Grand Rapids, MI 49525   www.gospelcom.net/calvarychurch

This large church has extensive family ministries and a large single adults program; small groups; senior adult activities; assimilating and discipleship ministries; Festival of Lights Christmas program reaches more than 20,000; Saturday night service.

TRINITY REFORMED CHURCH
1224 Davis Avenue NW
Grand Rapids, MI 49504   616-451-4131
        www.reformed.net/rca/mi/gr/trinity/trinity.html

Hillsdale

CAMBRIA BAPTIST CHURCH
2772 Lilac Road   517-357-4343
Hillsdale, MI 49242   http://cambriabaptist.cjb.net

HILLSDALE FIRST UNITED METHODIST CHURCH
45 North Manning Street
Hillsdale, MI 49242   517-437-3681

Creative sermons; warm, relaxed, relevant worship services; strong midweek children's ministry; Home Development ministry visits elderly and shut-ins.

Hudsonville

FAIR HAVEN MINISTRIES
2900 Baldwin Street   616-662-2100
Hudsonville, MI 49426   www.fhmin.org

Large suburban church's Young Seekers ministry pairs youth with adult members; 285 in pastoral elders ministry who work with families; music ministry includes choir and orchestra.

Kalamazoo

THIRD REFORMED CHURCH
2345 North Tenth Street   616-375-4815
Kalamazoo, MI 49009   www.thirdreformed.org

Rapidly growing, diverse congregation with many ministries, including high school, college, women's, singles, children's, and youth; several choirs and musical ensembles.

Midland

FIRST BAPTIST CHURCH OF MIDLAND
915 East Sugnet
Midland, MI 48642   517-835-6731

Temperance

CROSSROADS COMMUNITY CHURCH
1590 West Temperance Road   734-847-4135
Temperance, MI 48182   www.excitingchurch.com

Worship services connect with the unchurched through music and drama; Biannual New Community Institute disciples members; encourages all members to discover and use their spiritual gifts; small groups; children's and youth programs.

MINNESOTA
Eden Prairie

WOODDALE CHURCH
6630 Shady Oak Road   952-944-6300
Eden Prairie, MN 55344   www.wooddale.org

Contemporary and traditional services include drama and faith stories; outreach programs for seekers; small groups; classes; mentoring for spiritual growth of members.

Mahtomedi

ST. ANDREW'S LUTHERAN CHURCH
900 Stillwater Road   651-426-3261
Mahtomedi, MN 55115   www.saintandrews.org

Large church with a variety of ministries, including youth, children, Communion, welcoming ministry, and numerous fellowships; strong community outreach; sister relationship with a church in Slovakia; senior housing; day school.

Minneapolis

MOUNT OLIVET LUTHERAN CHURCH
5025 Knox Avenue South   612-926-7651
Minneapolis, MN 55419   www.mtolivet.org

Cathedral of the Pines camp develops faith for children and young adults; on the hour Christmas, Ash Wednesday, Good Friday, and Easter services afford multiple options; All Sportsmen's Dinner with first-class speakers honors young student/athletes.

PILGRIM BAPTIST CHURCH
5100 James Avenue North
Minneapolis, MN 55430   612-529-9186

Moorhead
TRINITY LUTHERAN CHURCH
210 Seventh Street South, Box 188   218-236-1333
Moorhead, MN 56560   www.trinitymhd.com

Four handbell choirs and seven vocal choirs participate in a traditional worship; offers recovery and support groups; extensive
youth services; men's fellowship.

Oronoco
DOUGLAS UNITED METHODIST CHURCH
6507 Seventy-fifth Street NW
Oronoco, MN 55960   507-281-3526

Sunday school outreach ministers to neighborhood children,
emphasizes music and fun; Bible study groups; biblical preaching;
caring fellowship.

Ramsey
LORD OF LIFE LUTHERAN CHURCH
14501 Nowthen Boulevard NW   763-427-1100
Ramsey, MN 55303   www.lol.org

Crossroads service for youth; Impact Life groups help teens deal
with life issues; Leadership Institute trains members; traditional
blended with comtemporary services at this large, growing,
seeker-sensitive suburban church.

Rochester
GOOD SHEPHERD LUTHERAN CHURCH
559 Twentieth Street SW
Rochester, MN 55902   507-289-1748

PEOPLE OF HOPE
1816 Second Street SW   507-280-9766
Rochester, MN 55902   www.peopleofhope.com

Ethnic and economically diverse church with informal, contemporary worship services; outdoor worship center for summer

services; numerous small groups that care for the community and the congregation.

MISSISSIPPI
Madison
CHAPEL OF THE CROSS
674 Mannsdale Road
Madison, MS 39110   601-856-2593

Moss Point
WADE BAPTIST CHURCH
20623 Highway 63
Moss Point, MS 39562   228-588-3356

This family- and community-oriented church is growing rapidly; strong children's programs and music ministry.

MISSOURI
Ellisville
ST. JOHN'S LUTHERAN CHURCH
15808 Manchester Road   636-394-4100
Ellisville, MO 63011   www.stjohnsellisville.org

Large suburban church with creative, energetic worship; down-to-earth, practical teaching; hosts major Christian artists and concerts; strong youth programs; emphasis on small groups for both members and church staff.

Kansas City
GRACE UNITED CHURCH
811 Benton Boulevard
Kansas City, MO 64124   816-231-5745

Food pantry program supplies more than 450 families monthly; Peacemaking Academy summer program teaches nonviolence and cultural awareness; youth employment project; Hispanic ministry; urban training center; worship reflects multicultural congregation.

PALESTINE MISSIONARY BAPTIST CHURCH
3619 East Thirty-fifth Street
Kansas City, MO 64128   826-921-6009

Two apartment buildings for senior citizens provide meals and activities; two day care centers for preschoolers; emphasizes evangelism.

ST. ANDREW'S EPISCOPAL CHURCH
6401 Wornall Terrace
Kansas City, MO 64113 816-523-1602

VINEYARD CHRISTIAN FELLOWSHIP OF KANSAS CITY NORTH
8341 NW Mace Road, Suite 101 816-746-5454
Kansas City, MO 64152 www.hometown.aol.com/vcfnorth

Worship service with contemporary music, casual atmosphere, practical messages; small groups led by lay ministers meet every day of the week; community outreach and service.

NEBRASKA
Lincoln
ST. MARK'S UNITED METHODIST CHURCH
8550 Pioneers Boulevard 402-489-8885
Lincoln, NE 68520 www.stmarks.org

Programs for all ages; pet ministry; many sports programs; emphasizes lay leadership and disciple building.

NEW JERSEY
Bloomfield
BROOKDALE BAPTIST CHURCH
1350 Broad Street 973-338-8536
Bloomfield, NJ 07003 www.brookdalebaptist.com

Hackettstown
GATHERING PLACE FOURSQUARE CHURCH
493 U.S. Highway 46E
Hackettstown, NJ 07840 908-813-8777

Morristown
CHURCH OF THE REDEEMER
36 South Street
Morristown, NJ 07960 973-539-0703

Various social outreach programs include a soup kitchen, hospitality network, and the Eric Johnson House, which provides housing and services for people with HIV/AIDS; communications ministry; many parish life activities and pastoral care ministries.

Neptune
COMMUNITY BAPTIST CHURCH
424 Lakewood Road
Neptune, NJ 07753   732-775-5093

Newark
ST. JAMES A.M.E. CHURCH
588 Dr. Martin Luther King Boulevard   973-622-1344
Newark, NJ 07103   www.stjamesamenwk.com

Many outreach programs, including housing, soup kitchen, Thanksgiving meal, and Christmas toy giveaway; credit union; prayer ministry; ministries for men, women, children, and youth.

NEW MEXICO
Albuquerque
HOFFMANTOWN CHURCH
8888 Harper Drive   505-828-2600
Albuquerque, NM 87111   www.hoffmantown.org

Large church with many small groups and classes; "Lunch with the Pastors" for new members; many discipleship and Bible study opportunities for all ages; casual, contemporary services as well as traditional.

NEW YORK
Brooklyn
THE BROOKLYN TABERNACLE
290 Flatbush Avenue   718-783-0942
Brooklyn, NY 11217   www.brooklyntabernacle.org

A Grammy-winning choir; 24-hour-a-day intercessory prayer groups; powerful Tuesday evening prayer ministry; intercultural and intergenerational.

LAFAYETTE AVENUE PRESBYTERIAN CHURCH
85 South Oxford Street   718-625-7515
Brooklyn, NY 11217   www.cloud9.net/~pofn

Cultural Crossroads, Inc., an outreach group overseen by the church, offers gospel music, dance classes, and art training; People of Faith network addresses social justice issues; parents cooperative playgroup gives relief for parents and children.

Fredonia

HARVEST CHAPEL FREE METHODIST CHURCH
39 Matteson Street
Fredonia, NY 14063   716-679-0987

Offers Life Discovery Series courses that focus on conversion, discipleship, and missions; various small groups; engaging and energetic worship.

Harlem

ABYSSINIAN BAPTIST CHURCH
132 West 138th Street   212-862-7474
New York, NY 10030   www.adcorp.org/abyssinianchurch.htm

This African American congregation founded in 1808 plays a major role in the socioeconomic revitalization of Harlem; programs, some partnered with other agencies, include family services, housing, neighborhood cleanup, and education and youth development.

Horseheads

MARANATHA BIBLE CHAPEL
774 Sing Sing Road
Horseheads, NY 14845   607-739-7168

Jamaica

ALLEN A.M.E. CATHEDRAL
110-31 Merrick Boulevard   718-206-4600
Jamaica, NY 11433   www.allencathedral.org

Large African American church with 6,600 attending; excellent Christian school; sponsored the building of more than 160 two-family homes; church-run investment clubs educate members about the market.

Mt. Kisco

Mt. Kisco Presbyterian Church
605 Millwood Road   914-666-8305
Mt. Kisco, NY 10549   www.mkpc.org

Many significant outreach ministries include programs for people recovering from substance abuse; church school for children; provides housing and care for senior citizens and retirees.

New York City

First Presbyterian Church
12 West Twelfth Street   212-675-6150
New York, NY 10011   www.firstpresnyc.org

History of progressive, socially conscious leadership in its community; members volunteer in many community agencies; adult education classes and church school for children on Sunday mornings; emphasis on quality music.

Jan Hus Presbyterian Church
351 East Seventy-fourth Street   212-288-6743
New York, NY 10021   www.janhuspresbyterian.beliefnet.com

This small but active congregation works for both local and international social justice causes; its homeless outreach program provides counseling, work training, and legal aid; many 12-step recovery groups meet at the church each week.

Metro Baptist Church
410 West Fortieth Street
New York, NY 10018   212-594-4464

Worship reflects the diversity of multicultural membership; oversees a not-for-profit agency as an umbrella for community ministries and development; houses volunteer missions and ministry teams working in New York City.

Overseas Chinese Mission
154 Hester Street
New York, NY 10013   212-219-1472

Faith ministry aimed at evangelizing Chinese immigrants through local and global ministries.

ST. BARTHOLOMEW'S EPISCOPAL CHURCH
109 East Fiftieth Street   212-378-0200
New York, NY 10022   www.stbarts.org

This landmark church offers a variety of adult education classes; small groups; weeknight worship service; community ministries; counseling center; outstanding music programs.

Sayville

NEW LIFE COMMUNITY CHURCH
380 Lakeland Avenue   516-589-5890
Sayville, NY 11782   www.new-life-church.org

Sponsors many community events to promote servant evangelism; adult ministries include Bible studies, meetings, and dinners; small-group communities; food ministry delivers food to church and community families.

NORTH CAROLINA
Black Mountain

ST. JAMES EPISCOPAL CHURCH
424 West State Street   828-669-2754
Black Mountain, NC 28711   www.stjameswnc.org

Excellent community outreach programs; offers extensive support and recovery groups.

Brevard

ST. TIMOTHY UNITED METHODIST CHURCH
P.O. Box 429   828-883-2985
Brevard, NC 28712   www.gbgm-umc.org/st-tim

Trained volunteers partner with families to provide financial stability and stronger self-esteem; lay caregiving ministry visits homebound; almost 50 percent of this congregation volunteers in the community.

Charlotte

HICKORY GROVE BAPTIST CHURCH
6050 Hickory Grove Road   704-531-4000
Charlotte, NC 28215   www.hgbc.org

More than 6,000 attend on Sunday at five services on two campuses; thriving Sunday school ministry; weekly evangelism training program.

MECKLENBURG COMMUNITY CHURCH
8335 Browne Road   704-598-9800
Charlotte, NC 28262   www.mecklenburg.org

Church with more than 2,500 in attendance; weekend seeker services; home-based small groups.

WAREHOUSE 242
1213 West Morehead Street, Suite C   704-344-9242
Charlotte, NC 28208   www.warehouse242.org

See chapter 9.

Hendersonville
HENDERSONVILLE FIRST BAPTIST
312 Fifth Avenue West
Hendersonville, NC 28739   828-693-3493

MUD CREEK BAPTIST CHURCH
403 Rutledge Drive   828-692-1262
Hendersonville, NC 28739   www.mudcreekchurch.org

Exciting, high-energy ministry for youth; blended music and worship; care ministries contact more than 3,300 monthly.

Sandy Ridge
DELTA UNITED METHODIST CHURCH
2080 Delta Church Road
Sandy Ridge, NC 27046   336-871-9622

OHIO
Akron
CORNERSTONE FREE METHODIST CHURCH
578 Killian Road
Akron, OH 44319   330-644-3937

Cincinnati

COLLEGE HILL PRESBYTERIAN CHURCH
5742 Hamilton Avenue   513-541-5676
Cincinnati, OH 45224   www.chpc.org

Pastors visit church small groups to pray with members and gather feedback; lay people care for members who are hurting; extensive ministries to the congregation and the church's community.

MOUNT AUBURN PRESBYTERIAN CHURCH
103 William Howard Taft Road   513-281-5945
Cincinnati, OH 45219   www.mtauburnpresby.org

Emphasis on leading a Christlike life; many social justice organizations are housed in the church building; weekly fellowship following worship service.

VINEYARD COMMUNITY CHURCH
11340 Century Circle East   513-671-0422
Cincinnati, OH 45246   www.cincyvineyard.com

This diverse congregation stresses service and evangelism; worship services give practical, biblical messages; helps newcomers assimilate quickly through small groups.

Cleveland

OLIVET INSTITUTIONAL BAPTIST CHURCH
8712 Quincy Avenue
Cleveland, OH 44256   216-721-3585

Church with more than 3,000 members partnered with the medical community to create a medical center in its neighborhood that offers excellent holistic health care; active outreach ministry; dynamic worship services; couples ministry.

PILGRIM CONGREGATIONAL UNITED CHURCH OF CHRIST
2592 West Fourteenth Street
Cleveland, OH 44113   216-861-7388

Strong peace and justice ministries; ministry to gays and lesbians; church is home to two theater companies and a program that brings quality music programs free to its urban community.

Columbus

VINEYARD SOUTHWEST
1159 Demorest Road 614-274-3697
Columbus, OH 43204 www.vineyardsw.org

Three Sunday worship services; two youth groups; many small groups and adult education classes; "Martha Ministries" creative outreach projects.

Medina

CORNERSTONE CHAPEL
3939 Granger Road 330-723-3334
Medina, OH 44256 www.cornerstonechapel.org

Cutting Stones Bible study group for ages 18–30; King's Kids motorcycle club; cell groups; Psalmist School of Music and Fine Arts for homeschooled children.

Toledo

CALVARY ASSEMBLY OF GOD
5025 Glendale Avenue 419-381-0254
Toledo, OH 43614 www.toledocalvary.org

Wednesday night family program; choir, orchestra, and drama ministries; counseling ministry; home care groups and discipling classes; Christian school for infants through sixth grade.

OKLAHOMA
Lone Wolf

LUTHERAN MINISTRIES OF SOUTHWEST OKLAHOMA
P.O. Box 368 580-846-5459
Lone Wolf, OK 73655 www.lutheranok.com

See chapter 1.

Oklahoma City

CHURCH OF THE SERVANT
14343 North MacArthur Boulevard 405-721-4141
Oklahoma City, OK 73143 www.umcservant.org

Megachurch with a care ministry involving more than 700 lay people; hundreds of members take part in national and international missions; numerous small groups offer extensive biblical and theological training.

Tulsa

HIGHER DIMENSIONS FAMILY CHURCH
8621 South Memorial Drive   918-250-0483
Tulsa, OK 74133   www.higherd.org

Large, multiethnic congregation; Raven's Nest ministry provides enough food for a week for more than 300 families monthly; strong children's ministry; Family Life Enrichment Center provides counseling and support.

RHEMA BIBLE CHURCH
P.O. Box 50126   918-258-7191
Tulsa, OK 74150   www.rhema.org/rbc.htm

Dynamic worship with large choir; youth ministry; ministry to prisoners and the sick; weekly worship services broadcast; Bible correspondence school.

VICTORY CHRISTIAN CENTER
7700 South Lewis Avenue   918-491-7700
Tulsa, OK 74136   www.victorytulsa.org

More than 11,000 attend this multicultural megachurch; about 850 cell groups; missions and international Bible schools; large Christian school.

OREGON
Lake Oswego

CHRIST CHURCH PARISH
1060 Chandler Road   503-636-5618
Lake Oswego, OR 97034   www.ccparish.org

Traditional and contemporary services; four-year education for ministry program; singles fellowship; parish nurse; strong youth program; outreach programs support local, national, and international ministries.

Portland

CITY BIBLE CHURCH
9200 NE Fremont Street   503-255-2224
Portland, OR 97220   www.citybiblechurch.org

Extensive intercessory prayer ministry; business ministry teaches godly principles in business; Christian Leadership Training Institute; dramatic arts ministry; programs for singles, women, seniors, and children; K–12 school.

FIRST PRESBYTERIAN CHURCH OF PORTLAND
1200 SW Alder Street   503-228-7331
Portland, OR 97205   www.fpcpdx.org

Neighborhood revitalization programs include affordable housing and child development center; Operation Nightwatch ministers to homeless and lonely people; Food Box works with mentally ill, homeless, and addicted people; houses refugee families.

PENNSYLVANIA
Bethel Park

CHRIST UNITED METHODIST CHURCH
44 Highland Road   412-835-6621
Bethel Park, PA 15102   www.christumc.net

This dynamic church in the suburbs offers creative outreach programs that include a Sunday night contemporary service, seeker-sensitive service, and cable TV ministry; adult Bible studies; various choirs and musical groups; thriving small-group ministry.

Gettysburg

GETTYSBURG FOURSQUARE CHURCH
328 West Middle Street   717-334-5410
Gettysburg, PA 17325   www.gettysburgfoursquare.org

Fellowship groups; congregational nursing ministry; free clothing bank; mission and aid projects to Russia.

Philadelphia

THE AFRICAN EPISCOPAL CHURCH OF ST. THOMAS
6361 Lancaster Avenue
Philadelphia, PA 19151   215-473-3065

Shepherding ministry cares for entire congregation; strong sense of stewardship allows for multiple outreach programs; thriving ministries to senior citizens.

CHINESE CHRISTIAN CHURCH AND COMMUNITY CENTER
225 North Tenth Street
Philadelphia, PA 19107   215-627-2360

WOODLAND BAPTIST CHURCH
2210 South Sixty-fifth Street
Philadelphia, PA 19142   215-729-0214

Pittsburgh

ALLEGHENY CENTER ALLIANCE CHURCH
250 East Ohio Street   412-321-4333
Pittsburgh, PA 15212   www.acac.net

Worship and preaching on social and economic issues; Christian community development through Urban Impact Foundation with parent training, mentoring, and job readiness; intercultural children and youth ministries foster respect between diverse groups.

Reading

FIRST PRESBYTERIAN CHURCH
37 South Fifth Street
Reading, PA 19602   610-375-3389

Growing urban church that offers blended and traditional worship services; Sunday school programs for all ages; Wednesday night family suppers followed by age-appropriate programs.

West Lawn

GLAD TIDINGS ASSEMBLY OF GOD
1110 Snyder Road
West Lawn, PA 19609   610-678-0266

Senior pastor teaches weekly welcome class for visitors interested in church membership; youth programs emphasize real-life

application of the Bible; a variety of classes include singles, married, seniors, grief groups, and divorce.

Wexford
ORCHARD HILL CHURCH
2551 Brandt School Road
Wexford, PA 15090   724-935-5555

Weekend seeker services with contemporary music, video, and
drama; small-group communities; Wednesday evening worship
with Bible study.

SOUTH CAROLINA
Columbia
TRINITY EPISCOPAL CATHEDRAL
1100 Sumter Street
Columbia, SC 29201   803-771-7300

Greenville
FIRST BAPTIST CHURCH
847 Cleveland Street   864-233-2527
Greenville, SC 29601   www.fbcgvlsc.com

Pastoral counseling service; media center with 10,000 items
available; 300 members participate in 10 choirs.

SOUTH DAKOTA
Sioux Falls
OUR SAVIOR'S LUTHERAN CHURCH
909 West Thirty-third Street   605-336-2942
Sioux Falls, SD 57105   http://inst.augie.edu/church/OSL

Large church offers two contemporary and three traditional
services weekly; variety of care ministries include a parish nurse
and monthly Communion to the homebound; many outreach
programs and support groups.

TENNESSEE
Cleveland
FAITH MEMORIAL CHURCH
910 Seventeenth Street NW
Cleveland, TN 37312   423-476-6281

Ongoing community assistance program; "Little People's Church" has its own building and pastor; annual toy giveaway for children.

Cordova

BELLEVUE BAPTIST CHURCH
2000 Appling Road   901-385-2000
Cordova, TN 38018   www.bellevue.org

C.A.R.E. network ministers to people with painful life issues; weekly breakfast for businesspeople; Academy for Christian Training and Service offers concentrated, practical, Bible-based classes.

Fayetteville

FAYETTEVILLE ARP CHURCH
1720 Huntsville Highway
Fayetteville, TN 37334   931-433-5205

Gallatin

FIRST PRESBYTERIAN CHURCH
167 West Main Street
Gallatin, TN 37066   615-452-3151

Hendersonville

FIRST BAPTIST CHURCH
106 Bluegrass Commons Boulevard   615-824-6154
Hendersonville, TN 37075   www.1st-baptist.org

Excellent preaching is relevant to the community; strong children's ministries; quality staff and lay leadership.

Memphis

MISSISSIPPI BOULEVARD CHRISTIAN CHURCH
70 North Bellevue   901-729-6222
Memphis, TN 38104   www.mbccmemphis.org

Large, inner-city African American church offers 70 ministries that serve the congregation and the community; Christian Academy provides an Afro-centric, academically challenging curriculum for preschool through sixth grade.

Nashville

BELLEVUE PRESBYTERIAN CHURCH
100 Cross Timbers Drive
Nashville, TN 37221   615-646-1666

FIFTEENTH AVENUE BAPTIST CHURCH
1203 Ninth Avenue North
Nashville, TN 37208   615-256-4334

HOBSON UNITED METHODIST CHURCH
1107 Chapel Avenue
Nashville, TN 37206   615-228-7334

Full-time after-school and summer programs for neighborhood youth; conflict resolution program works with teenagers and adults; variety of outreach ministries to the community.

TEMPLE BAPTIST CHURCH
3810 Kings Lane
Nashville, TN 37218   615-876-4084

A large, welcoming African American congregation; provides meals, clothing, and medical and dental screening to the homeless and unemployed; after-school ministries to at-risk youth; offers individual and group counseling at off-campus center.

UNA CHURCH OF CHRIST
1917 Old Murfreesboro Pike   615-361-8920
Nashville, TN 37217   www.unachurch.org

Offers many ministry opportunities, including worship, computer ministry, benevolence, fellowship and welcoming, and community outreach; adult education for all ages at Sunday and Wednesday Bible classes.

Old Hickory

OLD HICKORY CHURCH OF CHRIST
1001 Hadley Avenue
Old Hickory, TN 37138   615-847-2386

Provides worship services, Bible classes, transportation, and other help to large retirement home; produces newsletter for families as well as seminars and free tapes; extensive support for India missions.

TEXAS
Amarillo
SOUTHWEST CHURCH OF CHRIST
4515 Cornell Street   806-352-5647
Amarillo, TX 79109   www.southwestcofc.org

Arlington
MT. OLIVE BAPTIST CHURCH
301 West Sanford Street
Arlington, TX 76011   817-274-3644

Austin
UNIVERSITY UNITED METHODIST CHURCH
2409 Guadelupe   512-478-9387
Austin, TX 78705   www.uumc.org

Large church with traditional worship offers extensive family events and programs for children; ministries to college students; outreach to homeless families.

Carrollton
PRINCE OF PEACE
4000 Midway Road   972-447-9887
Carrollton, TX 75007   www.princeofpeace.org

A variety of programs and ministries; young adult and student ministries; adult ministries include Bible classes, prayer chains, worship, and celebration arts ministries; small groups for newcomers.

Dallas
THE EPISCOPAL CHURCH OF THE TRANSFIGURATION
14115 Hillcrest Road   972-233-1898
Dallas, TX 75240   www.transfiguration.net

Neighborhood-based ministries; AIDS outreach ministry; lay Eucharist ministry to those unable to attend services; hospitality groups reach out to visitors, new members, and absentees; many fellowship groups; adult education.

FRIENDSHIP WEST BAPTIST CHURCH
616 West Kiest Boulevard   214-371-2029
Dallas, TX 75224   www.friendshipwest.org

New membership orientation and First Friends Ministry help bring newcomers into the church community; mentoring; drama and dance ministries and Soul Stirrers Institute are some of the dozens of programs at this predominantly African American church.

NORTHWAY BAPTIST CHURCH
3877 Walnut Hill Lane   214-357-4391
Dallas, TX 75229   www.northwaybaptist.org

Adult education classes in leadership, family development, evangelism, and Christian growth; dynamic and innovative worship service for youth; counseling and pastoral care; several choirs and instrumental ensembles; children's ministry.

PEACE MENNONITE CHURCH
11001 Midway Road   214-902-8141
Dallas, TX 75229   http://web2.airmail.net/pmc

Monthly fellowship meals; Sunday school for all ages; many community volunteer opportunities at this small church.

ST. LUKE "COMMUNITY" UNITED METHODIST CHURCH
5710 ERL Thornton Freeway, P.O. Box 150425   214-821-2970
Dallas, TX 75315   http://stlukecommunityumc.org

Welcoming African American traditional worship; four choirs offer extensive opportunities for music ministry; Bible study groups; media and computer ministries; AIDS ministry.

ST. MICHAEL AND ALL ANGELS
8011 Douglas Avenue
Dallas, TX 75225   214-363-5471

Pathways to Ministry program encourages younger vocations in the Episcopal Church; provides food, tutoring, and other services to inner-city Dallas at the church's Jubilee Center; eight varied worship services each Sunday.

Duncanville

JUBILEE UNITED METHODIST CHURCH
301 Frank Keasler Boulevard   972-283-2264
Duncanville, TX 75116   www.theloveclinic.com/jubilee.html

Hosts the Love Clinic, a contemporary relationship ministry that addresses issues such as divorce, singleness, and marriage; offers a 36-week Disciple Bible Study that covers the entire Bible; active youth ministry.

Eagle Pass

REDEEMER EPISCOPAL CHURCH
648 Madison Street
Eagle Pass, TX 78852   830-773-5122
                    www.dreamwater.com/redeemer/redeemer.htm

English and Spanish services are offered at this historic church.

Houston

BRAESWOOD ASSEMBLY OF GOD
10611 Fondren Road
Houston, TX 77096   713-777-1651

Large racially and ethnically diverse church with a welcoming spirit; every worshiper encouraged to join a small-group Bible study.

BRENTWOOD BAPTIST CHURCH
13033 Landmark Street   713-852-1400
Houston, TX 77045   www.brentwoodbaptist.org

Large African American congregation sponsors 10 mission churches; large variety of ministries includes short-term housing for teenage mothers with AIDS, a food pantry, criminal justice ministry, an Alzheimer's program, and employment assistance ministry.

LAKEWOOD CHURCH
7317 East Houston Road   713-635-4154
Houston, TX 77028   www.lakewood.cc

Recognized as a diversified congregation with a national television broadcast; supports missions all over the world; sends videotapes to more than 100 countries; average of 12,000 attend Sunday morning services.

SAGEMONT BAPTIST CHURCH
11323 Hughes Road   281-481-8770
Houston, TX 77089   www.sagemontchurch.org

A megachurch that offers extensive opportunities for singles, men, women, and youth; homeless outreach; clowning ministry; bus ministry provides transportation; counseling services.

ST. JOHN'S UNITED METHODIST CHURCH
2019 Crawford Street   713-659-3237
Houston, TX 77002   www.gbgm-umc.org/stjohns-houstontx

Large-scale daily meals program for the homeless; health clinic; emotionally powerful worship; preschool and elementary school; many community services such as job readiness training and computer education; committed to economic development.

SECOND BAPTIST CHURCH
6400 Woodway   713-465-3408
Houston, TX 77057   www.second.org

Small-group ministry is the basis of this megachurch; two campuses offer parenting classes and Bible study; care and growth groups assist people with emotional and spiritual needs.

WINDSOR VILLAGE UNITED METHODIST CHURCH
6000 Heatherbrook Drive   713-723-8187
Houston, TX 77085   www.kingdombuilder.com

Large African American church offers a range of classes, Bible studies, and concerts; Kingdom Builders Prayer Institute teaches believers how to pray; job services programs; help for small businesses; lay counseling provides spiritual support.

Kerrville

FIRST BAPTIST CHURCH
625 Washington
Kerrville, TX 78028   830-257-5033

Extensive outreach program includes special events, visitation, small groups, and neighborhood outreaches; strong music program; traditional and contemporary Sunday morning services; 90 percent of service attenders also in Sunday morning Bible studies.

TRINITY BAPTIST CHURCH
800 Jackson Road   830-895-0100
Kerrville, TX 78028   www.tbck.org

Deeply involved with local and national missions; small Bible study groups offered weekly.

Plano

CHRIST EPISCOPAL CHURCH
4550 Legacy Drive   972-618-0222
Plano, TX 75024   www.christchurchplano.org

This large church focuses on discipleship; strong worship, small-group programs, and children's ministry.

Rockwall

FIRST BAPTIST CHURCH
610 South Goliad Street
Rockwall, TX 75087   972-722-8371

San Antonio

CONCORDIA LUTHERAN CHURCH
16801 Huebner Road   210-479-1477
San Antonio, TX 78258   www.concordia-satx.com

Music is a strong element of worship services; many weekly Bible studies and topical studies; school for K–8 and day care for infants to 4 years old; ministries for all ages.

NEW CREATION CHRISTIAN FELLOWSHIP
12525 Nacogdoches   210-646-7997
San Antonio, TX 78217   www.nccfonline.org

Services broadcast on TV and radio; Christian school for K–5; church bookstore provides high quality Christian electronic and print media; women's resource center; early learning center for infants to 6 years old.

ST. PAUL'S EPISCOPAL CHURCH
1018 East Grayson   210-226-0345
San Antonio, TX 78208   www.stpauls-satx.org

Second oldest Episcopal congregation in San Antonio maintains "high church" tradition and emphasizes outreach; Our Lord's Table food distribution ministry serves 150 neighborhood families; provides several events annually for neighborhood children.

Stafford

THE VINEYARD CHURCH OF SUGARLAND/STAFFORD
5015 Grove West Boulevard   281-240-8463
Stafford, TX 77497   www.slvineyard.org

Growing church with home-based small groups; ministries to men and women; children's and youth programs; arts ministry; Sunday evening Life Development classes; offers Alpha courses to introduce people to the Christian faith.

Victoria

FAITH FAMILY CHURCH
P.O. Box 4528   361-573-2484
Victoria, TX 77903   www.ffcvictoria.org

Large church with a mix of Caucasians and Hispanics; reality-based Sunday teaching; more than 100 ministries and 100 small groups.

PARKWAY BAPTIST CHURCH
4802 John Stockbaugher Drive
Victoria, TX 77904   361-572-8368

Sunday morning services target the unchurched; more than 100 small groups meet in people's homes; 70-plus ministries.

Waco

CALVARY BAPTIST CHURCH
1001 North 18-A   254-753-6446
Waco, TX 78208   www.cbcwaco.com

Sunday morning Bible study for all ages; Wednesday night ministry to inner-city children and youth; lay-led children's ministries.

UTAH
Park City
PARK CITY COMMUNITY CHURCH
4051 Highway 224   435-649-8131
Park City, UT 84098   www.ditell.com/~pccc

Encourages congregational involvement in many community programs; youth fellowship; adult and children's choirs; mid-week Bible studies; small-group fellowship.

VIRGINIA
Alexandria
CHRIST CHURCH
118 North Washington Street   703-549-1450
Alexandria, VA 22314   www.historicchristchurch.org

Historic church is a popular tourist attraction but maintains a vital and active faith community; strong local and international outreach programs; vibrant weekly youth groups; growing small-group program.

Ashland
ATLEE COMMUNITY CHURCH
11179 Hopson Road, Suite 7   804-798-5333
Ashland, VA 23005   www.atleechurch.org

Sunday seeker service; small groups; music, drama, and other arts enrich Sunday services; student ministry offers small groups and monthly worship services; New Community midweek worship service.

Hampton
CALVARY COMMUNITY CHURCH
2311 Tower Place   757-825-1133
Hampton, VA 23666   www.calvarycommunity.org

Generation Ministries disciples children and youth; Calvary Christian Academy offers programs through middle school;

Community Unity Day reaches out with opportunities and information on counseling, employment issues, and self-esteem.

Lynchburg

THOMAS ROAD BAPTIST CHURCH
701 Thomas Road   804-239-9281
Lynchburg, VA 24514   www.trbc.org

The CENTER outreach program provides tutoring, mentoring, teaching, and fellowship for families; extensive youth ministries; Gatekeepers ministry for men; partnered with church plant project in Chicago.

Norfolk

FIRST BAPTIST CHURCH OF NORFOLK
312 Kempsville Road   757-451-3226
Norfolk, VA 23502   www.firstnorfolk.org

Wide variety of Bible classes stress practical lessons; faith evangelism training.

FIRST LUTHERAN CHURCH
1301 Colley Avenue
Norfolk, VA 23514   757-625-1953

ROCK CHURCH OF NORFOLK
1301 East Little Creek Road
Norfolk, VA 23518   757-480-5411

ST. PAUL'S EPISCOPAL CHURCH
201 St. Paul's Boulevard
Norfolk, VA 23510   757-627-4353

Welcomes and integrates newcomers; strong liturgy with a rich offering of music, preaching, silence, and sacramental traditions; youth program.

Steele's Tavern

OLD PROVIDENCE PRESBYTERIAN CHURCH
1005 Spottswood Road
Steele's Tavern, VA 24476   540-377-6706

Sterling

RIVERSIDE PRESBYTERIAN CHURCH
21010 Southbank Street, PMB 510   703-444-3528
Sterling, VA 20165   www.riversidechurch.com

Growing youth group offers quality small groups and exciting events; variety of music groups; community outreach includes disaster response team and work with many community agencies.

Vienna

VIENNA PRESBYTERIAN CHURCH
124 Park Street NE   703-938-9050
Vienna, VA 22180   www.viennapres.org

Offers a contemporary Saturday evening worship and fellowship; youth involved in national and international missions; adult education series; small covenant groups.

Virginia Beach

VINEYARD COMMUNITY CHURCH
4444 Expressway Drive   757-424-4444
Virginia Beach, VA 23464   www.vineyardchurch.com

Extensive mail outreach vital to this congregation located in a highly transient area of the country; high involvement in women's ministries; intensive follow-up program for new Christians.

WASHINGTON
Gig Harbor

CHAPEL HILL PRESBYTERIAN CHURCH
P.O. Box 829   253-851-7779
Gig Harbor, WA 98335   www.chapelhillpc.org

Inquirers class with weekend retreats required for membership; core groups; nine-month disciple-making ministry; blended worship; extensive young adult ministry; performing arts ministry.

Kenmore

NORTHLAKE LUTHERAN CHURCH
6620 NE 185th Street   425-486-6977
Kenmore, WA 98028   www.northlakelutheran.org

Youth and parents active in local and international missions; programs for families and seniors; Thursday Bible studies.

Monroe
Sky Valley VCF
317 Butler Street   360-794-7749
Monroe, WA 98272   www.skyvalvcf.org

Evening and morning Sunday services; Kidz Church for kindergarten through fifth grade; home-based small groups; women's intercessory prayer; high school program.

Renton
Renton Bible Church
973 Union Avenue NE
Renton, WA 98059   425-226-3590

Gives almost one-third of its budget to overseas and retired missionaries; active Awanas program for children and teenagers.

Seattle
Chinese Baptist Church, Seattle
5801 Beacon Avenue South   206-725-6363
Seattle, WA 98108   www.seattlecbc.homepage.com

One-hundred-year-old intergenerational Chinese-based congregation offers traditional and contemporary services in Chinese and English.

Christian Faith Center
21204 Twenty-fourth Avenue South
Seattle, WA 98198   206-824-8188

Church of Mary Magdelene
811 Fifth Avenue
Seattle, WA 98111   206-621-8474

Church for women and children only; weekly worship for homeless and formerly homeless women; strong choir.

Evangelical Chinese Church
651 NW Eighty-first Street   206-789-6380
Seattle, WA 98117   www.eccseattle.org

More than 100 children in children's worship and Sunday school; well-structured adult Sunday school with well-trained teachers; pays half of all travel expenses for summer short-term overseas mission projects; English, Cantonese, and Mandarin services.

JAPANESE BAPTIST CHURCH
160 Broadway
Seattle, WA 98122   206-622-7351

MARS HILL FELLOWSHIP
7758 Earl Avenue   206-706-6641
Seattle, WA 98117   www.marshillchurch.org

Cutting-edge postmodern church emphasizes living in community; small groups; weekly cross-cultural Bible study and fellowship; social action committee works to meet people's physical and spiritual needs; parenting and marriage classes.

TRINITY LIFE CENTER
4402 South Graham Street
Seattle, WA 98118   206-722-9288

UNIVERSITY CONGREGATIONAL CHURCH
4515 Sixteenth Avenue NE
Seattle, WA 98105   206-524-2322

UNIVERSITY TEMPLE UNITED METHODIST CHURCH
1415 NE Forty-third Street   206-632-5163
Seattle, WA 98105   www.gbgm-umc.org/utemple

An urban church in a university community that strives for inclusivity; Atlantic Street Center helps low-income minority families; MAPS care team offers support to people living with AIDS; food bank.

Spokane

WHITWORTH COMMUNITY PRESBYTERIAN CHURCH
312 West Hawthorne Road   509-466-0305
Spokane, WA 99218   www.whitpres.org

Growing suburban church has a variety of children's and youth ministries, including Bible-based teaching; increasing numbers of people involved in local, regional, and international ministries; small-group ministry.

WISCONSIN
Kaukauna
PEACE UNITED METHODIST CHURCH
2300 East Wisconsin Avenue
Kaukauna, WI 54130   920-766-3311

Wausau
FIRST UNITED METHODIST CHURCH
903 North Third Street
Wausau, WI 54403   715-842-2201

Rich music program includes children's, youth, and adult choirs; traveling missions store sells Third-World crafts to raise money for the artisans; strong education ministries for children.

Whitewater
FIRST UNITED METHODIST CHURCH
145 South Prairie Street
Whitewater, WI 53190   262-473-2131